EARLY JUDAISM

EARLY JUDAISM

BY

LAURENCE E. BROWNE, B.D.
S.P.G. RESEARCH STUDENT IN ISLAM

CAMBRIDGE
AT THE UNIVERSITY PRESS
1929

CAMBRIDGE
UNIVERSITY PRESS

University Printing House, Cambridge CB2 8BS, United Kingdom

Cambridge University Press is part of the University of Cambridge.

It furthers the University's mission by disseminating knowledge in the pursuit of education, learning and research at the highest international levels of excellence.

www.cambridge.org
Information on this title: www.cambridge.org/9781107438262

© Cambridge University Press 1920

First edition 1920
First published 1920
Reprinted 1929
First paperback edition 2014

A catalogue record for this publication is available from the British Library

ISBN 978-1-107-43826-2 Paperback

CONTENTS

INTRODUCTION

THE history of the Children of Israel is marked by three great interventions of the Lord for their salvation: first, the salvation of Israel from bondage in Egypt, secondly the salvation of the tribe of Judah from captivity in Babylon, and thirdly the salvation of both Jew and Gentile from the power of sin by the Messiah, our Lord Jesus. The first deliverance was in the main material, a deliverance from physical bondage, and it affected, as far as we know, every member of the Israelite race. The second deliverance was partly material and partly spiritual, because it was not only a political or social deliverance, but it also gave liberty for the practice of their religion. It only affected a certain proportion of the Jews, for the more materialistic among them preferred to abide in Babylon. The third deliverance was entirely spiritual, and affected only a small proportion of the Jews: it was only a small 'remnant' who accepted Jesus as the Messiah. For us who believe in Him it is one of the most striking facts of all history that He, the Saviour of the world, came of the Jews, and that yet to the Jews as a whole He proved a stumbling-block rather than a Saviour. It is unquestionable that the Jewish birth of our Lord ought to have been an advantage to the Jews, ought to have brought salvation very near to their doors. And as we do not believe in a God who acts by mere caprice, we must believe that His choice of Judaism as the earthly home of His incarnate Son was in accordance with a plan of salvation for the world in which Judaism was destined to play an important part. It is not here disputed that the doctrines of Judaism were made to a large extent the basis of the doctrines of Christianity.

The fact that the mass of the Jews failed to rise to the opportunities of Christianity gave St Paul "great sorrow and unceasing pain" in his heart, and indeed that must be the feeling of every Christian, whether of Israelite or Gentile birth, who sympathetically considers the story of the Chosen People. Failure there undoubtedly was, and failure cannot be predicated of God but only of men. For so great a failure as this, in face of the many promises of God, we must look not to the ordinary weaknesses of humanity, the hardness of heart and stiffness of neck which are to be found in every nation under heaven, but to some more definite rejection of God's will and to the adoption of some opposing principle. It would only be a superficial view of the case to suppose that the whole fault lay with the priests in Jerusalem, in the days of our Lord, who clamoured for His crucifixion. The principles which actuated their conduct did not originate in their life-time, but rather had their roots in past history. It is not sufficient to say that the people as a whole never rose to the spiritual heights of the prophets. It is not expected in any nation that the mass of the people should reach the level of their prophets. Nor is any fault to be found with the prophets, for verily they rose to some of the greatest heights of divine inspiration. The question that we ask is, Why did prophecy die out? The main purpose of this book is to enquire into the period when prophecy was dying out, and to consider how far the failure of Judaism was due to the religious and political principles which gained the upper hand at the very foundation of Judaism, *i.e.* in the sixth and fifth centuries B.C. when, under Persian suzerainty, a Jewish state was founded with its centre at Jerusalem on the site of the old Southern kingdom of Judah. Sir G. A. Smith[1] speaking of Judaea and her people has said, "At all times in which the powers of spiritual initiative or expansion were needed, she was lacking, and so in the end came her shame. But when the times required concentration, indifference to the world, loyalty to the past, and passionate patriotism, then Judaea took the lead, or stood alone in Israel, and these virtues even rendered brilliant the hopeless insane struggles of her end." We shall see that in the Persian period of her history Judah lacked the spiritual initiative and expansion which were needed to fulfil the task to which she had been called.

It will be hard for a Jew to read these pages, written from the standpoint of one who sees in Christianity the fulfilment of the hopes of ancient Israel. And yet I would humbly express the hope that what is written here may help the Jews in their Zionist aspirations of the present time. For there is danger lest this movement should be spoiled, even by those who have religion at heart, by a narrowness of outlook restricted to the children of Israel. Dr Gaster has recently said[2], "The Jewish Commonwealth is to give to the world a lead, not only in the new interpretation of ancient truths, but also in the practical application of the ancient laws, towards the solution of many of the social problems which so much oppress and darken the life of the inhabitants of Europe and America." And again he says[3], "Unless the religious spirit is allowed to take a new flight, and unless the Jews feel themselves to be

[1] *Historical Geography of the Holy Land*, p. 259.
[2] *Zionism and the Jewish Future*, ed. by H. Sacher (1916), p. 97.
[3] *Op. cit.* p. 98.

the messengers of God's truth, no gathering, no talking
of Jewish nationality has any meaning, or will have any
beneficial result either for the Jews or for the rest of the
world. The Jewish regathering is to be of great moment
in the history of the emancipation and progress of man-
kind. Only from this point of view has Zionism a
meaning and Judaism a justification." But in the very
same volume in which Dr Gaster has penned these fine
words, another writer, Nahum Sokolow, one of the most
ardent Zionists, painting the picture of a typical "New
Jew," makes him say[1], "Here (*i.e.* in Palestine), in joyous
industry, in struggle for life, I affirm myself among the
sons of earth, as a man after my own fashion. And
though I do not care much for missions to the world,
I think none the less that in this man-like shape the
world will understand me much better. Let them come
and see me. I am living Judaism." The Zionist movement to-day needs the "powers of spiritual initiative
and expansion" of which G. A. Smith spoke, as much
as they were needed at the return of the Babylonian
golah. In the latter they were lacking, as we shall see.
Will they be lacking again to-day, as they are apparently
in Sokolow's typical "New Jew"?

However, this book is an historical study, and not
directly concerned with the present day. But history
has its lessons. And this period of Jewish history has
a lesson, for Jews and Christians alike, that truth cannot
be held in a closed fist but will burn the hand of him
who tries to enclose it; that true religion is a living
and a growing organism, whose life depends upon its
continual expansion, and whose fate is determined if it
be allowed to become pot-bound.

[1] *Op. cit.* p. 233.

BIBLIOGRAPHY

ARNOLD, WILLIAM R.: "The Passover Papyrus from Elephantine," Journal of Biblical Literature, 1912, p. 1.

BARNES, W. E.: Haggai, Zechariah, and Malachi (Cambridge
Bible), 1917.

BATTEN, L. W.: Ezra and Nehemiah (International Critical
Commentary), 1913.

BOX, G. H.: Isaiah, 1908.

BROWN, DRIVER and BRIGGS: Hebrew Lexicon, 1907.

BUDDE, KARL: (1) "The So-called 'Ebed Yahweh Songs,"
American Journal of Theology, 1899, p. 499.

(2) "Zum Text der drei letzten kleinen Propheten," Zeitschrift
für alttestamentliche Wissenschaft, 1906.

CHEYNE, T. K.: (1) Article "Servant of the Lord," Encyclopaedia Biblica.

(2) Origin and Religious Contents of the Psalter, Bampton
Lectures, 1891.

(3) Introduction to the Book of Isaiah, 1895.

(4) Commentary on Isaiah, 2nd edition 1882, 3rd edition 1884.

(5) Jewish Religious Life after the Exile, 1898.

(6) "Critical Problems of the Second part of Isaiah," Jewish
Quarterly Review, October 1891.

CONDAMIN, ALBERT: Le Livre d'Isaïe, 1905.

COOK, S. A.: (1) Article "Jews: Old Testament History,"
Encyclopaedia Britannica, 11th edition, vol. XV.

(2) "Significance of the Elephantine Papyri for the History
of Hebrew Religion," American Journal of Theology, July
1915.

COWLEY, A. E.: (1) "Ezra's Recension of the Law," Journal of
Theological Studies, vol. XI., July 1910.

(2) Jewish Documents of the Time of Ezra, 1919.

DRIVER, S. R.: (1) Introduction to the Literature of the Old
Testament, 7th edition, 1907.

(2) Deuteronomy (International Critical Commentary), 1895.

DUHM, B.: Das Buch Jesaia, 1892 (Handkommentar zum
Alten Testament).

xii BIBLIOGRAPHY

FÜLLKRUG, G.: Der Gottesknecht des Deuterojesaja, 1899.
GIESEBRECHT, F.: Der Knecht Jahwes des Deuterojesaja, 1902.
GRÜNEISEN: Ahnenkultus, 1900.
GUTHE, H.: Geschichte des Volkes Israel, 3rd edition 1914.
GUTHE, H., and BATTEN, L. W.: Ezra and Nehemiah, 1901
(Sacred Books of the Old Testament).
HÖLSCHER, G.: Palästina in der persischen und hellenistischen
Zeit, 1903.
VAN HOONACKER, A.: (1) Les Douze Petits Prophètes, 1908.
  (2) Une Communauté Judéo-araméenne à Éléphantine en
  Égypte aux VIe et Ve siècles av. J.-C. (Schweich Lectures
  for 1914), 1915.
JUDEICH, WALTER: Kleinasiatische Studien, 1892.
KAUTSCH, E.: (1) Gesenius' Hebräische Grammatik, 28th
  edition, 1909.
  (2) Article "Samaritaner," Herzog-Hauck Protestantische
  Real-Encyclopädie.
KENNETT, R. H.: (1) The Servant of the Lord, 1911.
  (2) Composition of the Book of Isaiah (Schweich Lectures
  for 1909), 1910.
  (3) "Origin of the Aaronite Priesthood," Journal of Theo-
  logical Studies, vol. VI., January 1905.
KIRKPATRICK, A. F.: The Psalms (Cambridge Bible), 3 vols.,
  1891–
KITTEL, R.: Biblia Hebraica, 2nd edition, 1909.
KNOBEL, A.: Der Prophet Jesaia, 3rd edition 1861 (1st edition,
  1843).
KÖNIG, E.: The Exiles' Book of Consolation, 1899.
KOSTERS, W. H.: (1) "Deutero- en trito-jezaja," Theologisch
  Tijdschrift, 1896.
  (2) Die Wiederherstellung Israels (German translation by
  Basedow), 1895.
LOWTH, ROBERT, Bishop of London: Isaiah, 11th edition, 1835.
MARTI, KARL: Das Buch Jesaja, 1900.
MEYER, E.: (1) Die Entstehung des Judenthums, 1896.
  (2) Article "Persia," Encyclopaedia Britannica, 11th edition.
  (3) Der Papyrusfund von Elephantine, 1912.
  (4) "Zu den aramäischen Papyri von Elephantine," Sitzungs-

berichte der königlichen preussischen Akademie der Wissenschaften, 1911.

MITCHELL, H. G.: Haggai and Zechariah. SMITH, J. M. P.: Malachi. BEWER, J. A.: Jonah. In one volume (International Critical Commentary), 1912.

MONTEFIORE, C. G.: Lectures on the Origin and Growth of Religion (Hibbert Lectures), 1892.

MONTGOMERY, J. A.: (1) The Samaritans, 1907.

(2) "Present Tendencies in Old Testament Criticism," Biblical World, vol. XLIII., 1914.

MOULTON, J. H.: Early Zoroastrianism, 1913.

NÖLDEKE, TH.: Article "Persia," Encyclopaedia Britannica, 9th edition.

OESTERLEY and BOX: Religion and Worship of the Synagogue, 1911.

PRÁŠEK, J. V.: Geschichte der Meder und Perser, 1906.

ROTHSTEIN, J. W.: (1) Juden und Samaritaner, 1908.

(2) Die Nachtgesichte des Sacharja, 1910.

SACHAU, E.: (1) "Drei Aramäische Papyrusurkunde aus Elephantine," Abhandlungen der königlichen preussischen Akademie der Wissenschaften, 1907.

(2) Aramäische Papyrus und Ostraka aus einer jüdischen Militär-kolonie zu Elephantine, 2 vols., 1911.

SAYCE, A. H., and COWLEY, A. E.: Aramaic Papyri discovered at Assuan, 1906.

SCHRADER, E.: Keilinschriftliche Bibliotek, 1889–96.

SMITH, G. A.: (1) Historical Geography of the Holy Land, 3rd edition, 1895.

(2) Jerusalem, 2 vols., 1907–8.

(3) Isaiah, 1890.

SMITH, H. P.: Religion of Israel, 1914.

SMITH, J. M. P.: "Jewish Religion in the Fifth Century B.C.," American Journal of Semitic Languages, July 1917.

SPRENGLING, M.: "The Aramaic Papyri of Elephantine in English," American Journal of Theology, July 1917 and July 1918.

STAERK, W.: Aramäische Urkunden zur Geschichte des Judentums (Lietzmann's Kleine Texte), 1908.

TORREY, C. C.: Ezra Studies, 1910.

UNGNAD, A.: Aramäische Papyrus aus Elephantine, 1911.

WADE, G. W.: Isaiah (Westminster Commentary), 1911.

WELCH, A. C.: "Present Position of Old Testament Criticism," Expositor, 8th Series, vol. VI., 1913.

WELLHAUSEN, J.: (1) Prolegomena zur Geschichte Israels, 4th edition, 1895.

   (2) Israelitische und Jüdische Geschichte, 1907.

WILLRICH, H.: Judaica, 1900.

NOTE:—References to Scripture texts are always given to the chapter and verse of the Hebrew or Greek original. When the numeration is different in the English Versions it is given in brackets afterwards.

CHAPTER I

ISRAEL'S MISSIONARY VOCATION

FROM early times some Hebrew writers passed in thought beyond the boundaries of their own nation to consider the condition and future of other peoples. Abraham is depicted as leaving his home to seek a new land, not merely for the enjoyment of his own tribe, but in response to a command of God which had in view the happiness of all the families of the earth. Even in the times when, according to modern investigators, the Hebrews regarded Yahweh as the God of Israel, and not as the only God, they believed that He had an interest in the moral behaviour of the gentiles. This is evident from the story of Sodom and Gomorrah, according to which the cities of the plain were destroyed for the wickedness of their inhabitants and not for any wrong done to Lot or Abraham.

As the Hebrews learnt that Yahweh was the only God of all the world, their thoughts must have turned into the wide channels of God's purpose for the whole of humanity. It is quite possible that universalistic ideas were expressed boldly before the exile, but the passages which take up this point of view stand out so remarkably from their context that many commentators feel compelled to treat them as later additions. Such are Is. ii. 2–4 (= Micah iv. 1–3) "Many peoples shall go and say, Come ye, and let us go up to the mountain of Yahweh, etc.," Is. xix. 24, 25 "Blessed be

Egypt my people, and Assyria the work of my hands, and Israel mine inheritance," Amos ix. 7 "Have not I brought up Israel out of the land of Egypt, and the Philistines from Caphtor, and the Aramaeans from Kir?" and Jer. iii. 17 "At that time they shall call Jerusalem the throne of Yahweh, and all the nations shall be gathered unto it."

Such universalistic ideas became a steady light in the writings of Deutero-Isaiah. Before we can begin to use those prophecies we must try to decide some difficult questions as to authorship, integrity and date. It is not necessary to argue again the point now generally conceded that at least the main part of Is. xl.–lv. is the work of somebody writing towards the close of the Babylonian exile, that is, shortly before the conquest of Babylon by Cyrus, and encouraging the exiled Jews to make the most of the opportunity to return to Palestine which would shortly be offered. For want of any other name this anonymous writer is referred to as the Second Isaiah or Deutero-Isaiah. The universalistic idea comes out most strongly in the conception of עֶבֶד יהוה the Servant of the Lord. But it is just here that the integrity of the chapters is called in question, for the main sections dealing with the Servant of the Lord, xlii. 1–4, xlix. 1–6, l. 4–9 and lii. 13–liii. 12, are thought by many commentators to be the work of another author than Deutero-Isaiah. If that were the case, these so-called "Servant Poems" might be either earlier than Deutero-Isaiah and incorporated by him, or later than he, and interpolated into his work. But in any case, if they are not by the hand of Deutero-Isaiah, we must be careful not to interpret

the Servant of Yahweh in them by the description of
the Servant in Deutero-Isaiah's own writings. On the
question of the integrity of these passages, therefore,
hangs not only their date but also the interpretation
of the central figure, the Servant of Yahweh.

The burden of proof must of course rest upon those
who would remove the Servant Poems from their present context. The first argument is based on rhythm,
and this will no doubt be differently valued according
to the view held as to Hebrew rhythm. The first,
second and fourth of the Servant Poems are more or
less in trimeters, a rhythm occurring only rarely in
the rest of the book; but the metre of the third is
different, and approximates to the pentameter, which
is common in Deutero-Isaiah. But the rhythm alone
cannot be an argument for independent authorship,
because there is no reason why the author should not
fall into a particular rhythm when dealing with a
subject transcending the usual level of his thoughts.
The frequent change of rhythm in Deutero-Isaiah
makes this all the more possible.

A similar argument against the integrity of the
Servant Poems is that they can be cut out so easily
without destroying the train of thought. Even if this
were really the case it would not prove difference of
authorship: the book is not laid out in a regular
scheme, but is evidently a collection of prophecies,
not spoken or written all on the same day, but produced as the prophet was inspired. And who will be
surprised if it was only on a few occasions that his
soul was uplifted to the great conception of the Servant of the Lord? Marti writes, "If one says that

these pieces can easily be removed from their connexion, it is to be noticed that this is equally true of
other pieces, but that by doing so one tears the heart
out of Deutero-Isaiah, and wounds in the most vital
part the whole structure of his message of comfort[1]."

The real test that must be applied to the Servant
passages is whether they contain anything contradictory to the rest of Deutero-Isaiah's work, or anything which we have good reason to believe he could
not have written. It is asserted that the characteristics
of the Servant are different from those in the other
passages where he is mentioned. We must therefore
begin by tracing separately the teaching about the
Servant as given in the Servant Poems and in the
rest of Deutero-Isaiah.

The Idea of the Servant of Yahweh in Deutero-Isaiah outside the Servant Poems.

xli. 8, 9. Israel is Yahweh's Servant, being the seed
of Abraham the friend of God. Abraham was called
from the end of the earth, for the purpose that he,
i.e. his seed, should be God's Servant.

xli. 10–20. Israel, Yahweh's Servant, has no need
to fear the nations, for Yahweh will give Israel strength
and power to overcome the nations. The wilderness
will become a watered land, bearing trees, so that
Israel may return, and through this wonderful deliverance the nations will learn the might of Yahweh—
"that they may see and know and understand together
that the hand of Yahweh hath done this, and the Holy
One of Israel has created it."

[1] *Jesaja*, p. 361.

xlii. 5–9. Apart from the preceding verses (1–4) which are one of the Servant Poems, which for the present we ignore, it is not definitely stated who the person addressed in verse 6 is. But when we compare verse 6 "I, Yahweh, have called thee in righteousness and will hold (or 'have held') thy hand" (אני יהוה קראתיך בצדק ואחזק בידך) with xli. 9 "thou whom I have taken hold of...and called thee" (אשר החזקתיך ...קראתיך), and with xli. 13 "For I Yahweh thy God am holding thy right hand" (כי אני יהוה אלהיך מחזיק ימינך), there can be no doubt that the person addressed in xlii. 6 is the same as in xli., namely Israel, the Servant of Yahweh. The section xlii. 5–9 goes much further than xli. 8–20 in delineating the Servant's work. It begins in the same way by speaking of the call, and how the Servant is held firm in Yahweh's hand; but then, instead of the idea of the vanquished gentiles learning to recognize the hand of Yahweh in Israel's deliverance, we find the idea of Israel consciously bringing salvation to the world— "I give thee for a covenant of the people, for a light of the gentiles, to open the blind eyes, to bring out the prisoners from the dungeon, and them that sit in darkness out of the prison house." The expression "covenant of the people," ברית עם, has caused difficulty to commentators because they did not expect such a universalistic idea which could conceive of all the nations as one people. But the prophet was only treating the nations as if they were now what they were before the Confusion of Tongues—עַם אֶחָד, 'one people' (Gen. xi. 6). The same word for 'people,' but with the article, had just been used in verse 5 with the same meaning of 'the human race.' The "covenant of the people" means that the whole human family is to enter into a covenant with Yahweh just as Israel had entered into a covenant with Him at Sinai. Grammatically it is possible to translate verse 7 otherwise than is done above, viz. "opening the blind eyes, etc.," making God the subject instead of the Servant, and meaning Israel by the blind. But the ordinary English rendering is better, for after reading 'a light to the gentiles' we expect to find the gentiles described as 'blind eyes' and 'dwellers in darkness.' Verse 7 then continues the thought of Israel's mission to the gentiles which we found in verse 6. The idea of Israel's blindness is however also in the prophet's mind, for in *vv.* 16 and 18 the blind are certainly Israel. Such a conception of an imperfect man being given a work to do for other imperfect men is not new in Deutero-Isaiah. It is as old as Isaiah himself, who, when he was sent with a message to the Israelites, recognized that he himself was a man of unclean lips (Is. vi. 5). There can be little doubt that in developing his idea of the Servant of the Lord Deutero-Isaiah was greatly perplexed as to how imperfect Israel could be God's missionary to the gentiles.

xlii. 18–25. The text of verse 19 is doubtful, and it is even possible that the whole verse is a later addition; but in any case the statement it contains of the Servant being blind and deaf only expands what is said in *vv.* 18 and 20 where Israel is represented as blind and deaf. The pitiable state of the Israelites "robbed and spoiled...snared in holes...hid in prison houses" is a punishment inflicted by Yahweh, "against whom we have sinned, and in whose ways they would not walk, neither were they obedient to His teaching." It is important to notice the sinfulness of the Servant as here described.

xliii. 1–4. This chapter introduces a change: Israel had, it is true, sinned, but now Yahweh has redeemed him. It is not quite clear in what way Egypt, Ethiopia and Seba have been given as a ransom for Israel (*vv.* 3, 4), but somehow Israel's sin has been put away. The same thought appears again in xliv. 21–23, and there Israel is spoken of definitely as the Servant. From another point of view Deutero-Isaiah had declared that Israel had received already double punishment for his sins, and that therefore his sins were pardoned (xl. 2). Regarding the sinfulness or sinlessness of the Servant we must bear in mind that those states are not permanent. Deutero-Isaiah does not seem to be very far from the Pauline idea that when a sinner is forgiven by God, God no longer regards him as a sinner. The same thought of Israel's sin and forgiveness appears again in xliii. 22–26.

xliii. 7. A new characteristic of the Servant is contained in this verse—"everyone that is called by my name, for my glory did I create him."

xliv. 1–5. Chapter xliii. had ended with a threat against Israel for his sins, but now again Yahweh has completely forgiven him—so completely that He can give him the name of Jeshurun, 'The Upright.' Following on directly after the promise of blessings to Israel comes *v.* 5 with its prophecy of men of other

nations coming to join the commonwealth of Israel
and to accept Yahweh as their God. It is implied,
but not stated, that this is through the activity of
the Servant. "One shall say 'I am Yahweh's,' and
another shall be called by the name of Jacob, and
another shall mark his hand 'To Yahweh,' and shall
be surnamed by the name of Israel." With this may
be paralleled other passages in Deutero-Isaiah, viz.
xlv. 22, 23 "Look unto me and be saved, all the ends of
the earth.... Unto me every knee shall bow, every tongue
shall swear," xlix. 7 "Kings shall see and arise, princes
and they shall worship, because of Yahweh that is
faithful, even the Holy One of Israel who hath chosen
thee," li. 4, 5 "A law shall go forth from me, and my
judgment for a light of the peoples. In a twinkling
I will bring near my righteousness (reading אַרְגִּיעַ‎:

אַקְרִיב‎). My salvation is gone forth, and mine arms
shall judge the peoples; the isles shall wait for me,
and on mine arm shall they trust." As Marti says,
"For Deutero-Isaiah the boundary of Israel's religion
is the boundary of the world."

xlv. 14, 15. The text of these verses is not sufficiently certain to draw sure conclusions from them.
But it seems probable that the Egyptians, Ethiopians
and Sabeans are depicted as seeking Israel because
they recognize that Israel has the knowledge of the
true God.

xlix. 23 a. The thought here expressed of the
subjugation of the gentiles to the Jews is foreign
to the thought of Deutero-Isaiah, but is the sort
of idea largely current later. The whole section

in which it occurs probably belongs to a later time[1].

l. 10 can scarcely be addressed to heathen people, because Yahweh is spoken of as 'his God.' The people addressed are probably those Jews who are in ignorance of Yahweh, the same sort of people as those spoken of in Ps. lxxxii. 5. The Servant in that case must be not the whole nation, but the teachers or the godly few. This tallies much better with the time when Zerubbabel was spoken of as the Servant (Hag. ii. 23), and it may safely be concluded that the verse, or the reference in it to the Servant, is a later addition.

In li. 4, 5, which has already been mentioned, it is Israel's coming victory that will convince the gentiles of Yahweh's power.

In lv. 4 it is David, *i.e.* the Davidic king, as representative of the people Israel, who has been appointed as "witness to the peoples, a leader and commander to the peoples." It is still clearly Israel who will attract the peoples by his knowledge of God: "Behold thou shalt call a nation that thou knowest not, and a nation that knew thee not shall run unto thee, because of Yahweh thy God, and for the Holy One of Israel, for He hath glorified thee" (lv. 5).

The Idea of the Servant of Yahweh in the Servant Poems.

We turn now to the Servant Poems to see whether the picture of the Servant there given disagrees with

---

[1] See p. 124 ff.

or contradicts in any respect the collection of ideas that
we have already found elsewhere in Deutero-Isaiah.

The First Poem, xlii. 1–4.

　"Behold my Servant, whom I uphold (אֶתְמָךְ־בּוֹ),
　　My chosen in whom my soul delighteth.
　　I have put my spirit upon him;
　　He shall bring forth judgment to the gentiles."

　　　　Cf. xli. 8. "Thou Israel my Servant, Jacob, whom
　　　　　　　　I have chosen."

　　　　　　　10. "I will uphold thee" (אַף־תְּמַכְתִּיךָ).

　　　　　xliv. 3. "I will pour out my spirit upon thy
　　　　　　　　seed."

　　　　　xlii. 6. "I will give the...for a light of the
　　　　　　　　gentiles."

　　　　　li. 4. "My judgment for a light of the peoples."

　"He shall not cry nor lift up,
　　Nor make his voice to be heard in the street.
　　A bruised reed shall he not break,
　　And smoking flax shall he not quench."

　There is nothing elsewhere quite parallel to this,
describing the gentle method of the Servant's work,
but it is not necessarily inconsistent with what is said
elsewhere.

The Second Poem, xlix. 1–6.

　"Yahweh hath called me from the womb,
　　From the bowels of my mother hath He made
　　　mention of my name.
　　And He hath made my mouth like a sharp sword;
　　In the shadow of His hand hath He hid me."

Cf. xliv. 2, 24. "formed thee from the womb."

xliii. 1. "I have called thee by thy name."

li. 16.　"I have put my words in thy mouth,
　　　　And have covered thee in the shadow
　　　　of mine hand."

"And He said to me, Thou art my Servant,
Israel in whom I will glorify myself"

(אֲשֶׁר בְּךָ אֶתְפָּאָר)‎.

Cf. xliv. 21. "Remember these things, O Jacob,
　　　　And Israel, for thou art my Ser-
　　　　vant."

23. "For Yahweh hath redeemed Jacob,
　　　　And will glorify Himself in Israel"

(וּבְיִשְׂרָאֵל יִתְפָּאָר)‎.

"But I said, I have laboured in vain,
I have spent my strength for nought and vanity.
Yet surely my judgment is with Yahweh,
And my recompence with my God."

Cf. xl. 27. "Why sayest thou, O Jacob, and speak-
　　　　est, O Israel,
　　　　My way is hid from Yahweh, and my
　　　　judgment is passed away from my
　　　　God?"

"That formed me from the womb to be His Ser-
vant,
To bring Jacob again to Him,
And that Israel be gathered to Him."

The idea of Israel's activity in assisting the restoration of Israel does not find expression elsewhere in
Deutero-Isaiah. It is referred to in:

xlix. 18. "All these gather themselves together and
come to thee.

As I live, saith Yahweh, thou shalt surely
clothe thyself with them all as with an
ornament,"

but we shall see reason to date xlix. 14–26 later.

Note. It is not safe to use xlix. 8 "to raise up the
land, to make them inherit the desolate heritages," as
a parallel; because if the preceding stichos "I will pre-
serve thee, and give thee for a covenant of the people" is
a later insertion copied from xlii. 6, then these words referred originally to the work of Yahweh and not of Israel.

"I will also give thee for a light of the gentiles,

That thou mayest be my salvation unto the end of
the earth."

Cf. xlii. 6. "I will give thee...for a light of the
gentiles."

lv. 4. "I have given him for a witness to the
peoples."

lii. 10. "And all the ends of the earth shall see
The salvation of our God."

The Third Poem, l. 4–9.

"The Lord Yahweh hath given me the tongue of
them that are taught (לִמּוּדִים),

That I should know how to sustain (or 'to teach,'
reading לִרְעֹת) the weary with words.

[1]The Lord Yahweh hath opened mine ear.

[1]In the morning He wakeneth mine ear to hear as
they that are taught."

[1] Emended text.

Cf. li. 16. "And I put my words in thy mouth."

liv. 13. "And all thy children shall be taught

of Yahweh" (לְמוּדֵי יהוה).

lv. 4. "Behold I have given him for a witness
to the peoples,

A leader and commander to the
peoples."

"I was not rebellious, nor turned away backwards.

I gave my back to the smiters, and my cheeks to
them that plucked off the hair.

I hid not my face from shame and spitting."

Cf. xliv. 2. "Thou Jeshurun" (*i.e.* Upright).

li. 23.   "...them that afflict thee,

Which have said to thy soul, Bow down
that we may go over.

And thou hast laid thy back as the
ground, and as the street to them
that go over."

"And the Lord Yahweh will help me.

Therefore have I not been confounded."

Cf. liv. 4. "Fear not, for thou shalt not be ashamed,

Neither shalt thou be confounded."

The Fourth Poem, lii. 13–liii. 12.

There are many expressions of the sufferings of the
Servant, *e.g.*

liii. 3. "He was despised and rejected of men:

A man of sorrows and acquainted with grief."

Cf. xlii. 22. "This is a people robbed and spoiled,

....

They are for a prey, and none de-
livereth."

xlix. 7. "Thus saith Yahweh,
The Redeemer of Israel, his Holy One,
To him whom man despiseth, to him
whom the nation abhorreth,
To the servant of rulers."

The sufferings of the Servant were because of others;
and yet the pain was inflicted by Yahweh:

liii. 4. "Surely he hath borne our griefs and carried
our sorrows."

liii. 10. "Yet it pleased Yahweh to bruise him."

Cf. xlvii. 6. "I was wroth with my people,
I profaned mine inheritance,
And gave them into thine hand.
Thou didst show them no mercy,
Upon the aged thou hast laid
Thy yoke exceeding heavily."

The Servant was sinless:

liii. 9. "Although he had done no violence,
Neither was any deceit in his mouth."

Cf. xliii. 4. "Since thou hast been precious in my
sight,
(And) honourable, I have loved thee."

25. "I will not remember thy sins."

xl. 2. "For she hath received at Yahweh's
hand
Double for all her sins."

xliv. 2. "Thou Jeshurun" (Upright).

As the text stands at present liii. 8 says "For the
transgression of my people was he smitten." The
meaning of this is doubtful, since elsewhere in chap. liii.
the transgression seems to be only that of the gentiles.
It may refer to the sins of Israel which have now been

more than compensated for by the punishment inflicted
(cf. xl. 2, quoted above). Or it may be a wider use of
the word עַם for all the inhabitants of the earth as
Yahweh's nation, as in xlii. 5, 6 (see note above, p. 5).
Some commentators would emend עַמִּי into עַמִּים, 'the
peoples,' but all the versions support our text.

The result of the Servant's sufferings was the benefit
of the gentiles:

liii. 5. "He was wounded for our transgressions,
....
And with his stripes we are healed."

Elsewhere it is rather that Israel's delivery from
suffering by Yahweh will be the means of attracting
and benefiting the gentiles, *e.g.* xlix. 7:

"Kings shall see and arise,
  Princes and they shall worship,
  Because of Yahweh who has been faithful,
  Even the Holy One of Israel who hath chosen thee."

Cf. also li. 4, 5.

Finally the Servant will rise to new life and prosperity:

lii. 13. "He shall be exalted and lifted up and shall
             be very high."
liii. 10. "He shall see (his) seed; he shall prolong
             his days;
             And the pleasure of Yahweh shall prosper
             in his hand."

The parallels are numerous, cf.:

xl. 31. "They that wait on Yahweh shall renew
             their strength;
             They shall grow wings like eagles."

xliv. 3. "I will pour my spirit upon thy seed,
         And my blessing upon thine offspring."
xlv. 25. "In Yahweh shall all the seed of Israel be
         justified and shall glory."

No one can fail to see the special beauty and fulness
of expression of the Servant Poems, especially the last
one, and the many parallels that have been drawn
here still leave the Servant Poems in their place of pre-
eminence. But these parallels are surely sufficient to
show that there is no contradiction in the two pictures,
that no argument for the separate authorship of the
Servant Poems can be based on the theory that they
contain a different conception of the Servant from that
which is found elsewhere in Deutero-Isaiah. One
might perhaps go further, and say that the nature of
the parallels is such as can scarcely be explained except by common authorship. A copyist would have
copied the whole phrases more exactly, and would
hardly have been able to reproduce so many of the
expressions of his original without saying exactly the
same thing. And whether Deutero-Isaiah or the author
of the Servant Poems be considered the imitator, it
would have to be admitted that he was nearly as great
a man as the one whom he copied, or even a greater.
Great men do not usually mould their language so
closely to an earlier model.

It is further asserted that the religious ideas expressed in the Servant Poems belong to a later period
than the exile. Prof. Kennett even thinks that they
reflect the thoughts of the second century B.C. He
says[1], "Though in the Scriptures composed up to and

---

[1] *The Servant of the Lord*, p. 17.

including the time of Nehemiah there are occasionally seen flashes of a dim consciousness that the other nations of the world as well as Israel are the object of Jehovah's care, those flashes never develop into a steady light." Yet the quotations above, not only from the Servant Poems, but from the rest of Deutero-Isaiah, are sufficient to show that at least in one prophet there was a studied conviction of Yahweh's purpose of bringing light to lighten the gentiles. Again Kennett says[1], "It is impossible that during the Persian period the nation ever supposed that Jehovah had commanded or would command His Servant Israel to preach His law to the Gentiles; for the policy of Nehemiah had been to isolate Israel from the Gentiles." We shall have to return to this question later But it can now be said that proof is required that Nehemiah's policy was the policy, even in his day, of all the great men of Israel; and it is possible to believe that broader, more universal, views were held during the exile, but that they were narrowed and cramped into the legalism that developed after the Return. For the present we cannot let our estimate of what an exilic prophet may have written be prejudiced by the policy of his nation nearly a century later.

The burden of proof with regard to the authorship of the Servant Poems lies, as said above, with those who attack their integrity as part of Deutero-Isaiah's work. The arguments they have adduced do not appear to prove their case, so that, until fresh evidence is brought forward, we may treat the Servant Poems as part and parcel of Deutero-Isaiah's prophecies.

[1] *Op. cit.*, p. 54.

With the failure of this attempt to separate the
Servant Poems, there falls also a great mass of specu-
lation as to who was intended by the Servant of
Yahweh. Apart from xlix. 3 the Servant is not
definitely stated to be Israel in the Servant Poems, and
one passage could easily be cut out by the critical
scissors. Different commentators have suggested
Isaiah, Jeremiah, Zerubbabel, Eleazar (see II Macc.
vi. 18–31) and Job as the martyr whose portrait is
given as the Servant of the Lord. Duhm, unable to
fit the picture to any of these, still thought that it referred to some historical martyr of whom there is no
other record. The clinching argument against these
theories is in the suggestion of a resurrection. Was
there any historical individual who had died (liii. 9)
at the time when the words were written, but who was
to live again in prosperity and share booty with the
mighty (liii. 10, 12)? Kosters says[1], "What we know
of Israel's religious ideas and expectations in the time
in which the Servant passages had their origin, makes
it at least not easy to suppose that people should have
expected the resurrection of a martyr, who should afterwards see his posterity and live a long life."

Against the suggestion that the Servant is merely
and directly a prediction of our Saviour, as was
supposed by early Christian writers, and as is still
maintained by Fr. Condamin, Wade answers conclusively[2], "His sufferings and death are described as
already past (xlix. 4, l. 6, lii. 14, liii. 2–9), and it is only
his restoration and exaltation that are thought of as
still in the future."

[1] *Theologisch Tijdschrift*, 1896, p. 593.   [2] *Isaiah*, p. 346.

If we are prepared to admit that the Servant Poems are of common authorship with the chapters in which they are imbedded, we find, not once but many times, the statement that Israel is the Servant of Yahweh. There is however one serious difficulty that must be met if we are to accept this view, namely that in xlix. 5, 6 the Servant is distinguished from Israel, for it is said to be the Servant's task to restore Israel, and that in liii. 8 it is said that he was stricken for the transgression of "my people." Some have suggested that an ideal Israel is intended, *i.e.* an Israel as it might be, a creation of the prophet's fancy. But the suggestion has nothing to commend it: "It is obviously an actually existing power, and the suggestion that the ideal Israel should be outraged by the actual Israel is essentially meaningless[1]." The difficulty of liii. 8, "my people," has already been discussed (p. 14), and some possible solutions have been offered. But the great difficulty of how Israel could be called upon to restore Israel only arises through our looking at the nation from a later standpoint. Consider the political state of Israel during the exile. Who were Israel? There were some Jews in Egypt, there was a community in Judaea which had largely intermarried with non-Jews, there was the even more mixed community in Samaria, and there were the Jews living in Babylonia whose fathers had been transported thither by Nebuchadrezzar. This scattering of the Israelites, their intermarriage with foreigners, and the fact that the resultant half-caste Jews sometimes worshipped Yahweh and sometimes did not, made it very difficult to define

---

[1] Kosters, *Theologisch Tijdschrift*, 1896, p. 591.

the limits of Israel. In one sense Israel consisted of those of pure Israelitish blood only; in another sense there were to be added to these such of the half-castes as worshipped Yahweh. This latter probably was the present Israel as Deutero-Isaiah conceived it. It practically meant all or most of the Jews in Babylon and a goodly proportion of the Jews in Palestine. This was the actual Israel, but it was called to the restoration of a greater Israel which should include also such of the half-castes as at present worshipped heathen deities—for by their Hebrew blood they were bound already in covenant to Yahweh, even if they were ignorant of it—and then to the further work, extending beyond any blood relationship, of being the missionary to the whole world.

With the difficulties thus explained, and assured for certain that it was the great prophet of the Exile who penned all the words about the Servant of the Lord, and that he stated explicitly that Israel was the chosen Servant, we can turn to consider what exactly was the call which he addressed to his people.

Remember first the occasion. The better part of the children of Israel—the better in every way—were in Babylonia, where their fathers had been brought against their will. Many of the present generation were no doubt contented with their lot, but contented or discontented they had no liberty to return to Palestine. But history was being made rapidly; the conquests of Cyrus were the talk of every lip; the days of the Babylonian Empire were clearly numbered; and whether or no Deutero-Isaiah was the first to suggest that the conquest of Babylon by Cyrus would bring liberty to the Jews, all the Jews when they heard the prophecy would readily agree with its truth. Many doubtless would have no use for the new liberty, but all would recognize that the disabilities under which they had lived, already partially removed under the old régime (II Kings xxv. 27), would be done away with on the advent of the conqueror. The prophet's part was not so much to announce the coming liberty as to teach the people how to use it. The reversal of Israel's fortune was to him no mere accident but a gift from God, and indeed to his prophetic eye the whole career of Cyrus was ordained by God for this one purpose—the liberation of the chosen people. He therefore preached to the people, exhorting them to recognize this great deliverance as the working out of a world-wide divine purpose. With the instinct of a true man of God he saw that God's workings are conditioned by man's obedience and co-operation. God made possible the restoration of the nation of Israel; He removed the mountains and the valleys; He turned the wilderness into well-watered fields; but Israel must tread the highway; Israel must make an effort if Israel is to be once more a nation. To put it in plain words, the commonwealth of Israel would never be restored unless the Jews in Babylonia were willing to sacrifice their commerce and their financial prosperity for the national ideal. If they would do this a glorious future lay before them.

But the God of all the world could not restrict His view to the future of a single race. Israel was undoubtedly the chosen people of God. To them alone had been vouchsafed the revelation of His moral character and unity. But the choice of Israel was an election not to privilege but to service. "It is too light a thing that thou shouldest be my servant to raise up the tribes of Jacob, and to restore the preserved of Israel. I will also give thee for a light to the gentiles, that thou mayest be my salvation unto the end of the earth" (xlix. 6). The task which God set His chosen people was to include the gentiles in its scope. Israel was to become the missionary of the world. Some modern writers have tried to excuse the Israelites for not seeking the evangelization of the world. Was it practical politics, they ask, for the Jews to go to the gentiles and convert them by preaching the religion of Yahweh? Probably not; but if we look closely that was not exactly what the prophet called on them to do. They were not called upon to start a campaign of publicity to advertise the virtues of the Lord. "He shall not cry, nor lift up, nor cause his voice to be heard in the street. A bruised reed shall he not break, and the smoking flax shall he not quench: he shall bring forth judgment in truth" (xlii. 2). The great virtue of Yahweh, His truth, was to be told not by words but by His visible fidelity to His plighted word in delivering Israel. "Thus saith Yahweh, the Redeemer of Israel (and) his Holy One, to him whom man despiseth, to him whom the nation abhorreth, to a servant of rulers: Kings shall see and arise, princes and they shall worship, because of Yahweh who is faithful, the Holy One of Israel who hath chosen thee" (xlix. 7). This magnifying of Yahweh through the delivery of Israel is in contrast to the blaspheming of His name through the present piteous state of His people—"Now therefore what do I here, saith Yahweh, seeing that my people is taken away for nought? They that rule over them howl, saith Yahweh, and my name continually all day long is blasphemed " (lii. 5). Just as the Son of God was glorified by Lazarus raised from the dead (John xi. 4), just as St Paul's highest commendation was in the persons of the Corinthian Christians (II Cor. iii. 2), so Israel restored was to be the witness to the power and fidelity of Yahweh: "I have declared, and I have saved, and I have shown—and there was no strange God with you—therefore ye are my witnesses, saith Yahweh, and I am God " (xliii. 12).

In the first place then Israel's witness was merely passive, that they had received such a blessing at Yahweh's hand. This was enhanced by the quiet confidence in Yahweh that Israel showed in suffering "He was oppressed, yet he humbled himself and opened not his mouth; as a lamb that is led to the slaughter, and as a sheep that before her shearers is dumb; yea he opened not his mouth " (liii. 7); "I gave my back to the smiters, and my cheeks to them that plucked off the hair; I hid not my face from shame and spitting. For the Lord Yahweh will help me, therefore have I not been confounded; therefore have I set my face like a flint, and I know that I shall not be ashamed " (l. 6, 7). But Israel has yet an active work on behalf of the gentiles to perform. When the gentiles seek Yahweh they will come to Israel to learn of Him, "they shall fall down unto thee, they shall make supplication unto thee, saying, Surely God is in thee " (xlv. 14. Then it will be the duty of Israel to admit these gentiles into the holy commonwealth

"One shall say, I am Yahweh's, and another shall be called by the name of Jacob, and another shall mark his hand 'To Yahweh,' and be surnamed by the name of Israel" (xliv. 5). And then also there will be opportunity for Israel, who has learnt such lessons in the days of affliction, to teach and help those gentiles who come to him: "The Lord Yahweh hath given me the tongue of them that are taught, that I should know how to sustain (or 'to teach') the weary with words" (l. 4).

Such, in brief, was the call of God to the children of Israel, through the mouth of the unknown prophet —surely a call which was not in itself impossible to be obeyed. At least two centuries earlier it had been revealed to Israel that Yahweh was the God of the universe. Now came the logical sequence, that Israel was called to admit the gentiles to share in the worship of Yahweh. And Israel was to be judged according to the use he made of this revelation that was committed to him.

CHAPTER II

THE HISTORICAL DOCUMENTS

THE history of the Jews in the years succeeding the advent of Cyrus is by no means clear, and if we are to trace the attitude they adopted towards other nations we must first draw out as accurately as possible the historical course of events. The principal documents which we are to use are the prophecies of Haggai and Zechariah and the books of Ezra and Nehemiah. The literary problems presented by Ezra and Nehemiah are some of the most difficult in the Old Testament, and it is only natural that they should have been left aside while the problems connected with the earlier books of the Old Testament were being tackled. The result however has been that attempts to reconstruct the post-exilic history of the Jews have not been based on a thorough-going criticism of the important documents. In recent years a serious attempt to grapple with the problems has been made by Prof. C. C. Torrey of Yale; and if his conclusions prove satisfactory they must inevitably influence our conception of this period of Jewish history. His *Ezra Studies* have given a great stimulus to the task of delineating afresh the religious ideas of the Jews after the Exile. A noteworthy attempt had been made in 1898 by Prof. Cheyne in his lectures on *Jewish Religious Life after the Exile*, but in spite of Cheyne's brilliant scholarship and imagination that work is now seen to be far from

satisfactory because many of the foundations were not
securely laid.

We begin then with a consideration of the literary and
historical criticism of Ezra and Nehemiah. It will not
be necessary here to repeat in detail the work of Torrey,
which should be read in its entirety, but only to give a
short summary of it, and to deal rather more fully with
the few points in which his conclusions are questioned.

In the writings known as I and II Chronicles, Ezra
and Nehemiah, we have what professes to be a complete history from the creation to the fifth century B.C.
The history was written with a distinct motive, and
therefore the parts which were not of interest to the
Chronicler are omitted or summarily mentioned. Thus
the early part of the history is compressed into a mere
genealogy, while the period of the Babylonian Exile
is passed over in complete silence. The motive of the
Chronicler, to put it in few words, was to glorify
Judaism and Jerusalem. Earlier on there had been a
desire to glorify Jerusalem, when the prophets tried to
abolish the worship of Yahweh in the country high
places, and when the author of Deuteronomy declared
that no sacrifice might be offered except in Jerusalem.
But from those days to the time of the compilation of
Chronicles much had happened to Israel, and the most
remarkable change was the dispersion of the Jews in
foreign lands. Either forcibly or of their own free will
the Jews had been scattered all over the civilized
world. We know of the deportations to Babylon by
Nebuchadrezzar, and we know of the Jewish colonies
in Upper Egypt in the sixth and fifth centuries B.C.
During the Persian period this dispersion continued,

until in the Greek period, *i.e.* after Alexander the Great, the Jews in Judaea began to be numerically of small importance compared with the Jews in other lands. There was a danger that the scattered Israelites would cease to look on Jerusalem as the centre and joy of the whole earth. And worse than this the people of Samaria, who also worshipped Yahweh, had built a temple of their own on Mt Gerizim, and this bade fair to rival the temple at Jerusalem. It was with feelings of intense anxiety at the thought of these things that the Chronicler sat down to write his history of the world which gave the place of first importance to the Jewish people and the Jewish religion, and regarded Jerusalem and its temple as the pivot of the world. Chronicles, Ezra and Nehemiah are in reality one book, and indeed the careless scribe who separated them did not make a clean cut, but ended II Chron. in the middle of a sentence, and then in beginning Ezra repeated the last two verses which he had written in II Chron. It is however only with the period covered by Ezra and Nehemiah that we are concerned. In order to obtain the text of that portion of the Chronicler's work as it left his hand we have the following materials:

(*a*) A Greek version known as Ἔσδρας *a*, which is translated into English in our Apocrypha under the title I Esdras.

(*b*) A recension partly in Hebrew and partly in Aramaic, which is printed in our Hebrew Bibles, and is translated in our English Bibles under the titles Ezra and Nehemiah. To distinguish this recension we shall call it 𝕸.

(c) A Greek version of 𝕸 which appears in the Greek Old Testament under the title Ἔσδρας β. As this follows 𝕸 very closely it is not translated independently into English. This must not be confused with the book in our English Apocrypha called II Esdras which is translated from a Latin work in no way connected with our book.

There are also versions from Ἔσδρας β into other languages, such as the Latin Vulgate, which are not of great importance to us.

It has just been said that Ἔσδρας β follows 𝕸 very closely. This is not the case with Ἔσδρας a (our I Esdras) which consists of some parts of Chron., Ezr., and Neh., arranged in a different order, and with some additional matter, thus:

I Esdras i.	= II Chron. xxxv. 1–xxxvi. 21.
ii. 1–15	= Ezra i.
ii. 16–30	= Ezra iv. 7–24.
iii. 1–v. 6	= additional matter: the story of the Three Guardsmen.
v. 7–73	= Ezra ii. 1–iv. 5.
vi. 1–ix. 36	= Ezra v.–x.
ix. 37–55	= Neh. vii. 73–viii. 13a.

It will be noticed that I Esdras ends in the middle of a sentence, the words "and they were gathered together" (καὶ ἐπισυνήχθησαν) being the opening words of a sentence in Neh. viii. 13. The first words of I Esdras also "And Josiah held the passover" do not sound like the beginning of a book, and it is therefore thought that I Esdras is a fragment of a book which had been torn off at both ends.

What is the relation of I Esdras to 𝕸? It used to

be thought that some scribe had taken certain parts of 𝔥 and rearranged them, together with some additional matter, and called it I Esdras. But we find that in some cases I Esdras is right and intelligible when 𝔥 is wrong and unintelligible; and in one case I Esdras has preserved eighteen verses which have dropped out of 𝔥. Further, the story of the Three Guardsmen, I Esdr. iii. 1–v. 6, shows by its idioms that it was not written originally in Greek, but is a translation from Aramaic, so that this interpolation was made when the book was in Hebrew or Aramaic. These facts suggest that I Esdras is a Greek translation from a Hebrew and Aramaic book which differed in important particulars from the Hebrew and Aramaic book which we know as 𝔥. That is, the Hebrew-Aramaic book existed at one time in two recensions or editions which differed considerably from one another, the one being 𝔥, and the other being the text presupposed by I Esdras.

The methods of textual criticism must now be applied to these two texts, in the endeavour to suggest the original order of the text as written by the Chronicler. The test whether we have guessed aright will be whether we can suggest plausible reasons for the changes that took place in producing these two very different recensions.

Both Ezra-Nehemiah and I Esdras as they stand confuse the historical order of events. The original text which we are trying to get at should differ from both our extant recensions in being in such an order that we can at least say that it was possible for an intelligent chronicler to write it so. For instance, it can be

seen at once that the events dealing with Ezra which
are recorded in Neh. viii. are out of place in their
present position and are really connected with the
events of Ezr. viii.; and almost all critics agree that
the section Ezr. iv. 7–23, dealing with the building of
the city walls in the reign of Artaxerxes, is out of place
in its present context and belongs later in the history.

The following suggestion for the original order in
which the book stood when it left the hand of the
Chronicler is that proposed by Torrey, except for the
position of Ezr. iv. 7–23 to be referred to later.

> I and II Chron.
> Ezr. i.
> I Esdras iv. 47–56.
> I Esdras iv. 62–v. 6.
> Ezr. ii. 1–iv. 5, 24.
> Ezr. v. 1–viii. 36.
> Neh. vii. 70–viii. 18.
> Ezr. ix. 1–x. 44.
> Neh. ix. 1–x. 40 (E.V. x. 39).
> Ezr. iv. 7–23.
> Neh. i. 1–vii. 69.
> Neh. xi. 1–xiii. 31.

In order to show the possibility that this was the
original order it is necessary to trace the steps by
which our two recensions may have arisen. Some of
the main facts on which the above hypothesis is based
are (i) that Josephus used I Esdras and not our cano-
nical Ezra and Nehemiah; *i.e.* in the history of the
text I Esdras was earlier than our Ezra and Nehemiah, (ii) that there are very great differences in the
order of I Esdras and Ezra-Nehemiah, which must be

accounted for somehow, (iii) that Neh. vii. 70–viii. 18 is certainly out of place in Ezra-Nehemiah, and that Ezr. iv. 7–23 (= I Esdr. ii. 16–30) is in two different positions in the two recensions, and historically out of place in both, and (iv) the sections I Esdr. iv. 47–56, iv. 62–v. 6, which have been added to the text, supply some information which has clearly dropped out at this point.

The first step in the dislocation of the text was the removal of the section Neh. vii. 70–viii. 18 from its original position to a place after Neh. vii. 69. The reason for this change was that the scribe was misled by the superficial similarity between Neh. vii. 70–73[1] and Ezr. ii. 68–70. They are not really identical, the similarity being due merely to the Chronicler's habit of repeating his favourite formulae, but the superficial similarity is sufficient to have deceived many modern commentators as well as the Jewish scribe.

The second step in the dislocation of the text followed as a logical consequence of the first, for Neh. ix. 1–x. 40 (E.V. x. 39) presupposed the reading of the Law that had been described in Neh. viii. And therefore that section was also moved, and placed directly after Neh. viii. 18.

The next step was the introduction (in Aramaic) of the story of the Three Guardsmen, a narrative of the time of Darius III which originally had nothing to do with the Jews. By equating one of the three young men with Zerubbabel (I Esdr. iv. 13) the scribe made this story an introduction to the return of the Israelites

[1] Neh. vii. 69–72 in the critical editions of Kittel and of Ginsburg, verse 68 being omitted. The common printed Hebrew Bibles agree with the English numeration.

from Babylon. It was necessary to add a few connecting verses, I Esdr. iv. 43–46, 57–61. The interpolator also changed the name of Cyrus in I Esdr. iv. 47, v. 2, 6, to Darius. L. W. Batten[1] thinks that Torrey is acting very arbitrarily in supposing that this change of name took place; but there is one piece of almost conclusive evidence, viz. that the decree authorizing the bringing of cedar wood from Lebanon, I Esdr. iv. 48, is quoted in Ezr. iii. 7 (= I Esdr. v. 53, E.V. v. 55) as a decree of Cyrus.

At the same time, presumably also to give an introduction to the story of the Three Guardsmen, the section Ezr. iv. 7–23 was moved from its original position (wherever that may have been) to a position after Ezr. i. Absurd as this position is, in bringing Artaxerxes before Darius, that is actually where we find it in I Esdr. ii. 16–30.

Here the history of the text divides. In one copy the scribe noticed the incongruity of having Neh. vii. 73–x. 40 (E.V. x. 39) in the place it then occupied, and therefore he moved it back to a position after Ezr. x. But he did not move back the verses vii. 70–72 because they were too firmly imbedded in their new context. This recension was translated into Greek, and was the version known to Josephus. Part of it is preserved to us as Ἐσδρας α.

In another copy of the text a different change was made. The scribe determined to remove the story of the Three Guardsmen, which was obviously unworthy of its place. With it he cut out I Esdr. iv. 43–v. 6, part of which, as we have seen, belonged to the Chronicler's original work. With the absence of the story of

---

[1] *Commentary on Ezra and Nehemiah*, p. 9.

the Three Guardsmen the position of Ezr. iv. 6–24, dealing with opposition to building the walls, became quite untenable, and it was moved a little later, viz. after Ezr. iv. 5 which deals with opposition to building the temple. Thus was produced 𝕳, our Hebrew Ezra and Nehemiah.

It may now be asked, What was the original position of Ezr. iv. 6–23? Torrey thinks that it stood originally where it does now in 𝕳, assuming that the scribe who tried to put it back into a reasonable position succeeded in restoring it to its original place. But, unless the scribe had some written evidence to go upon, how could he possibly guess its original position? It is much more probable that the scribe simply put it after another record of opposition and before another Aramaic section. As a matter of fact there is every reason to think that there was an abortive attempt to restore the city walls before the time of Nehemiah (see Neh. i. 3), and therefore the most probable place for the section in the original story is just before Neh. i. With this one difference from the original order of the book as suggested by Torrey, we arrive at an order which an intelligent chronicler could have produced. That is, Ezr. i. to iv. 5 belongs to Cyrus' reign, Ezr. v. 1 to vi. 22 to Darius, and Ezr. vii. onwards to Artaxerxes. Apart from Torrey's assumption as to the original position of Ezr. iv. 6–23 there is no ground for saying that the Chronicler was ignorant of the order of the Persian kings.

In order to substantiate the theory here put forward that Ezr. iv. 6–23 did not originally stand where it stands in 𝕳, we must ask the questions: How did the text run before this insertion was made in Ezr. iv.? and what is the literary history of the inserted section? The following is a conjectural attempt to supply answers.

(1) In the original story, when Ezr. iv. 24 followed Ezr. iv. 5 it probably ran something like this:

> a (Heb.) *"to frustrate their purpose all the days of Cyrus king of Persia.* Then ceased the work of the house of God which is at Jerusalem, and it ceased *until the reign of Darius king of Persia.*
>
> a (Aram.) Now in the second year of Darius, Haggai and Zechariah etc."

This is almost what is preserved to us in I Esdr. v. 73, "to hinder the finishing of the building all the time that king Cyrus lived. So they were hindered from building for the space of two years until the reign of Darius. Now in the second year of Darius, Haggai and Zechariah etc."

(2) When the story of the Three Guardsmen was inserted before the Return, which was now made to appear in the reign of Darius instead of Cyrus as in the original story, it became necessary to explain why the permission of Cyrus was not sufficient, and why Zerubbabel had to seek fresh permission. For this reason Ezr. iv. 7–23 (opposition to wall-building in the reign of Artaxerxes) was moved from its original position and put after Ezr. i. After it the following was added, being suggested by the words of *a* as restored above, and being written in Aramaic because the Artaxerxes narrative and the story of the Three Guardsmen were both in Aramaic:

β (Aram.) "and the building of the temple in Jerusalem ceased until the second year of the reign of Darius king of Persia." I Esdr. ii. 30b.

(3) At the beginning of the Artaxerxes narrative there was added, possibly from an independent source, a short notice about opposition of Bishlam, Mithredath, Tabeel etc. in the reign of Xerxes. When these names were accidentally connected with the Artaxerxes narrative, the Xerxes narrative was so mutilated as to be senseless. In this mutilated form it has been preserved in 𝕸, but Ἔσδρας a omits it altogether.

(4) The story of the Three Guardsmen was cut out. With its absence there could be no sense in having the Xerxes and Artaxerxes narratives in the position they held. The obvious thing was to move them forward to a position just before the beginning of Darius' reign in Ezra v. 1 which was also in Aramaic. This was made all the easier because of the remarkable similarity between a (Heb.) and β (Aram.). The scribe left β where he found it at the end of the Artaxerxes section, and before that section he did not write the whole of a, but only the words printed in italics, because the rest was parallel to β. Having thus, in accordance with β, put in the second year of Darius' reign, he omitted it in v. 1 where it certainly existed in the original story, as we see from I Esdr. vi. 1 and as we should expect from the fact that it is in Haggai which the Chronicler was using.

Having now recovered the original form of the work as published by the Chronicler, as far as may be done by the methods of textual criticism, we turn to trace the records further back still, and to ask whence he got the information for his book.

We learnt above that the Chronicler wrote with a motive, *i.e.* he did not simply transmit the information he received, but he selected from it such information as he needed, and when necessary he did not hesitate to change it. A most striking instance of the latter is I Chron. xxi. 1 = II Sam. xxiv. 1. In Samuel it was written that Yahweh in His anger moved David to number Israel; but though such a thought was possible when men's ideas of God were elementary, it was not possible for one with the high spiritual ideas of the Chronicler, and he therefore boldly changed it into "And *Satan* stood up against Israel, and moved David to number Israel."

Ezr. iv. 8–vi. 18 and vii. 12–26 are written in Aramaic, whereas the rest of Ezra and Nehemiah is written in Hebrew. Hebrew had been the language spoken in Palestine by the Israelites, and they had probably learnt it from the Canaanites whom they dispossessed. Aramaic was originally the language of the parts N. and N.E. of Palestine, but it had gradually spread until in the Persian period it had become the language of all diplomatic correspondence between Persia, Babylonia, Egypt, Palestine, Phoenicia, and even far distant Carthage. In the time of the Hebrew kings Aramaic was unknown to the common people of Judaea. In the time of our Lord it was the language they ordinarily spoke, though some could speak Greek also, and Hebrew was then a dead language. It is difficult to speak with certainty about the fifth to the third centuries B.C., but most probably both languages were spoken, and Aramaic was gradually getting the upper hand. Anyhow Hebrew was still sufficiently known to be used for literary purposes. The book of Daniel shares with Ezra-Nehemiah the peculiarity of being partly in Hebrew and partly in Aramaic.

The Aramaic parts of Ezra include what purport to be copies of letters and decrees, but the decree recorded in Ezr. i. is in Hebrew. It is generally agreed that the Chronicler himself knew very little history, but it is frequently asserted that he has incorporated into his book real genuine documents of high historical value. The Memoirs of Nehemiah, *i.e.* the accounts in the first person of the doings of Nehemiah, seem to be such genuine documents, and to give us good history. The question then arises as to the Aramaic parts. These no doubt were excerpted from a book written in Aramaic. But was this the real verbal record of the letters, or was it a composition of a later time? Two methods may be adopted to try and find an answer to this question.

(1), by the language. The Chronicler wrote in the third century B.C., while the reigns of Cyrus, Darius and Artaxerxes were in the sixth and fifth centuries B.C. Can we tell by the kind of Aramaic whether it belongs to the fifth century or to the third? There is a difference of opinion. Driver says[1] that the Aramaic of Daniel is "all but identical with that of Ezra," and he dates Daniel after 300 B.C., but he does not express himself definitely as to the date of the Aramaic parts of Ezra. G. A. Cooke says[2], "The dates of the O.T.

[1] *Introd. to the Lit. of the O.T.*, p. 502 f.
[2] *A Text Book of North Semitic Inscriptions*, p. xix.

Aramaic cannot in all cases be determined; parts of
Ezra are probably as early as the fourth century B.C.,
Daniel was written in the second century B.C.," but he
nowhere states his reason for his date of the Aramaic
of Ezra, and is probably guided rather by literary
criticism of the book than by linguistic study of the
Aramaic. Of Aramaic inscriptions and papyri which
have been unearthed the ones which are in a dialect
most like the Old Testament Aramaic are those from
Nabataea and Palmyra which date from the first century B.C. to the third century A.D. Lately there have
come to light papyri in Aramaic from Elephantine in
Upper Egypt dated 408 B.C. Torrey has pointed out
that these papyri show in at least one respect an
earlier stage of Aramaic, in using ז as the first letter
of the relative and demonstrative pronouns instead of
ד which appears in Biblical Aramaic, in the inscriptions of Nabataea and Palmyra, and in the Targums.
From this Torrey concludes that the Aramaic of Ezra
cannot be as early as the fifth century. S. A. Cook
says, "In vocabulary, phraseology, and style the dialect [*i.e.* of the Elephantine papyri] closely resembles
that of the Aramaic portions of Ezra and Daniel. It
is however an older type of dialect; and the view that
it is, philologically speaking, earlier than Biblical
Aramaic has been strongly supported, and is not
seriously affected by the arguments brought against
it[1]."

(2), from general probability. The most improbable
of the decrees and letters is that of Cyrus in Ezr. i. 2,

[1] "Significance of the Eleph. Papyri for the Hist. of Heb. Religion,"
Amer. Jour. of Theol., July 1915, p. 348.

for it is quite inconceivable that Cyrus, even if he wished to conciliate the Jews, would have said that he had been given all the kingdoms of the earth by Yahweh. But that decree is in Hebrew, and might be condemned as not genuine even by those who accepted the other decrees, all of which are in Aramaic. It is however generally agreed that the decree of Ezr. vii. 12–26 is improbable, for it is in the highest degree unlikely that the Persian king would pay for the sacrifices at Jerusalem even if he paid for the restoration of the temple. Nor is it at all likely that he would allow Ezra such full powers to enforce the Jewish law on "all the people that are beyond the River." It may be that this letter is a mere invention, or it may be that the real letter has been embellished; but it is evident that we have not before us in these Aramaic parts faithful copies of official records. When we also remember that the Aramaic seems to be more probably late than early, we are inclined to conclude that the Aramaic book used by the Chronicler was composed not so very long before his own time. Torrey thinks that this conclusion makes the Aramaic source worthless; but that does not logically follow, for the Aramaic writer may well have had some historical facts on which he based these letters and decrees that he composed.

Next we consider the so-called Memoirs of Ezra, Ezr. vii. 27, 28, viii. 15–34, ix. It is clear that the whole of chapters vii.–x. is not the work of one man, for no single author would have described Ezra's arrival in Jerusalem in vii. 9 and then described in viii. 15 ff. how he made preparations to start the journey. It is there-

fore probable that the Chronicler was indebted to
some earlier source, but whether this was ancient and
reliable or not we have no means of telling other than
the internal evidence of the subject-matter.

Summing up then we may say that of the sources
used by the Chronicler, the Memoirs of Nehemiah are
reliable. The Memoirs of Ezra and the Aramaic
source are of uncertain date and authorship, though
certainly in their origin independent of the Chronicler.
We have no external evidence to prove their trust-
worthiness or untrustworthiness, and the only criterion
as to their value will be whether or no they fit in with
other historical data which we possess.

Of these data the chief are provided by the books
of Haggai and Zechariah. The former contains actual
prophecies of Haggai, but they were compiled by some
other person as Haggai is spoken of in the third person. Zechariah's prophecies (Zech. i.–viii.) were, on
the other hand, compiled by himself. In a few places
redactional glosses have concealed this fact, but originally Zechariah spoke of himself in the first person.
The text of Zech. is in some places in rather a bad
state: notice for instance that in chap. i. verses 7 and 8
do not fit together. The only really serious difficulty
of a literary character in either of the two books
is in Hag. ii. 10–19. André tried to get over it
by supposing that the whole of that section is an
interpolation. That is not a satisfactory solution, and
has not been accepted by any other writers. A new
suggestion was made by Rothstein in 1908, that this
section was merely displaced from its original position, and this suggestion removes all the difficulties

and throws a great deal of fresh light on the period. We shall return to this subject in the next chapter.

It only remains to point out that the Chronicler made use of the books of Haggai and Zechariah. One may note, for instance, in Ezr. v. 1 that he was ignorant of the name of Haggai's father, since it is not given in Hag., but he gives Zechariah's father as Iddo who is mentioned as his grandfather in Zech. i. 1. Ezr. v. 1–5 is a piece of history written by the Chronicler, and his information was gained exclusively from Hag. and Zech. and from the Aramaic letter of Tattenai which follows (Ezr. v. 6–17). This fact will explain a curious error in Ezr. v. 4 which commentators have been at a loss to account for. That verse reads, "Then spake *we* unto them after this manner," when one would expect "Then spake *they* unto them after this manner." This remark, together with the preceding question about the author of the decree, is simply copied from Tattenai's letter (Ezr. v. 9, 10) and there of course Tattenai speaks in the first person. From this may be drawn the rather important conclusion that the Aramaic source contained letters and decrees, but no intervening history. The Chronicler wrote Ezr. v. 1–5 himself as an introduction to the letter he was about to insert, but he had no information beyond what the letter itself contained and what he learnt from Hag. and Zech. Another example of the Chronicler's use of Zech. is seen in Ezr. i. 1 (= II Chron. xxxvi. 22). The previous verse, II Chron. xxxvi. 21, had referred to Jeremiah's prophecy that the land should be desolate seventy years (Jer. xxix. 10). The Chronicler goes on to say that the prophecy was fulfilled by the rise of Cyrus. But how could he say that the prophecy was fulfilled, since 586 B.C. (destruction of the temple) to 537 B.C. (second year of Cyrus) is only 49 years? It was through a careless misunderstanding of Zech. Zechariah knew that the temple was not restored till the reign of Darius, and so he spoke of the seventy years as being fulfilled in the second year of Darius (Zech. i. 12) or the fourth year of Darius (Zech. vii. 5), which would make 66 or 68 years—near enough to the 70 years as a round number. The Chronicler thought that the restoration of the temple dated from the second year of Cyrus, but he copied Zechariah's statement about the seventy years without noticing that it did not agree with the second year of Cyrus.

CHAPTER III

THE RESTORATION

DEUTERO-ISAIAH judged rightly that when Cyrus conquered Babylon the deported Jews would be given liberty to return to their own land. The cylinder of Cyrus shows that such a policy of toleration was adopted towards all captive peoples. "The gods, who dwelt in all parts, deserted their dwellings in anger because Nabunaid had carried them away to Babylon. Marduk went round to all the dwellings (*i.e.* the people) whose homes were laid low, and he allowed the people of Šumir and Akkad, who were like corpses, to turn.... He permitted the return of all of the lands." "All gods, which I have returned to their towns, shall daily proclaim before Bel and Nebo the length of my days, and shall declare the word of my grace, and shall thus speak to Merodach my lord 'Cyrus the king etc.[1]'"

---

[1] Schrader: *Keilinschriftliche Bibliotek.* Inschrift auf dem Thoncylinder des Cyrus Königs von Babylon-Persien, 538-529 v. Chr. "Die Götter, welche alldorten wohnten, verliessen ihre Wohnungen in Zorne (darüber), dass er (d. h. Nabû-nâ'id) (sie) (die fremden Götter) nach Šuanna (Babylon) geführt hatte. Marduk war umhergegangen zu der Gesammtheit der Wohnungen (hier = Leute), deren Wohnsitze niedergelegt waren, und die Leute von Šumir und Akkad, welche Leichen glichen, er liess wenden..., bewilligte die Rückkehr der Gesammtheit aller Länder." "Alle Götter, welche ich in ihre Städte zurückgeführt habe, mögen täglich vor Bel und Nebo die Länge meiner Tage verkünden, mögen aussprechen das Wort meiner Gnade, und zu Merodach, meinem Herrn, mögen sie sprechen also : Cyrus der König usw."

It was the opinion of the Chronicler that the Jews took advantage at once of this opportunity to return to Jerusalem. He gives two versions of the decree which he supposed Cyrus had written granting special permission to the Jews to return to Jerusalem. The first of the two is in Hebrew, Ezr. i. 2–4, and in it Cyrus says that he has received all the kingdoms of the earth from Yahweh, and has been commanded by Yahweh to build the temple at Jerusalem. He therefore exhorts all Jews to return to Jerusalem for this purpose, and exhorts other people to help them with free-will offerings. The second version of the decree, Ezr. vi. 3–5, is in Aramaic, and directs the building of the temple and its dimensions, and orders the expenses to be paid out of the king's house. The sacred vessels also are to be restored. According to the Chronicler the vessels were conveyed by one Sheshbazzar (Ezr. i. 8, 11), and the Aramaic section v. 14–16 says further that this Sheshbazzar laid the foundation of the temple.

The view of the Aramaic source seems to have been that a return was made in the reign of Cyrus under Sheshbazzar, and that the temple was begun then, and that the work of building continued without intermission up to the time of Darius when it was completed. Note Ezr. v. 16 "Then came that Sheshbazzar and laid the foundations of the house of God in Jerusalem; and since that time even unto now hath it been building (מִתְבְּנֵא) and yet it is not completed." Turning to the book of Haggai we learn that the foundation of the temple was first laid in the second year of Darius. This is stated in Hag. i. 15. It is stated again in our present text in Hag. ii. 18, but that verse, as we shall see, is doubtful, and therefore we must not use it as a proof. But the whole of Haggai's first sermon, i. 2–11, suggests forcibly that no work had been done towards restoring the temple, and that when the work was begun it was at the instigation of Haggai. It is almost inconceivable that he would have spoken thus if a beginning had been made in the reign of Cyrus. He would have said rather, "You made a good beginning; why have you not continued?" Now, whatever may be the date of the compilation of Hag., the words of Haggai himself are contemporary evidence, and we have no difficulty in deciding to choose his evidence and to reject the later evidence of the Aramaic source. Historically the temple was not founded till the reign of Darius.

We have seen that the Chronicler was using Hag. and Zech. as well as the Aramaic source. How was he to reconcile the two statements as to the date of the foundation of the temple? He preserved both, by supposing that a foundation had been made in Cyrus' reign, but that the work had been interrupted, and that a fresh start was made in Darius' reign. The way he treated his material is seen from his description in Ezr. iii. 12 of how the old folk wept at the sight of the temple at its foundation in Cyrus' reign; for this description is evidently based on the words of Haggai at the founding of the temple in Darius' reign: "Who is left among you that saw this house in its former glory? and how do ye see it now? is it not in your eyes as nothing?" (Hag. ii. 3). By analogy we may guess that his account of the Samaritan offer of help in building the temple, and the opposition of the

people of the land, Ezr. iv. 1–5, is not unhistorical, but
was transferred to Cyrus' reign from its real occasion
in the reign of Darius. Followed, as has already been
suggested[1], by the words, "Then ceased the work of
the house of God which is at Jerusalem; and it ceased
until the reign of Darius king of Persia," a complete
explanation was offered of the necessity for a fresh
beginning. It should be said that it suited the Chronicler's frame of mind well to suppose that the Jews had
taken the first opportunity to return to their land and
to lay the foundations of the temple. He probably
gave in his original work the exact date of the return
to Jerusalem. I Esdr. v. 5, 6, as restored by Torrey,
reads, "And there rose up with him (*i.e.* with Jeshua)
Zerubbabel, son of Shealtiel, of the house of David,
of the lineage of Perez, of the tribe of Judah, in the
second year of the reign of Cyrus king of Persia, in
the month Nisan, on the first day of the month." Then,
with the intention of further magnifying this first return he inserted the long list of Ezr. ii., which he also
inserted later in his work (Neh. vii.), which shows
clearly by its contents that it was not simply a list of
the first party of returned exiles. The names of eleven
leaders are given, including Zerubbabel, Jeshua, and
Nehemiah, and not including Sheshbazzar. Moreover
the chapter concludes with lists of laymen, *vv.* 59, 60,
who could not prove their Israelite descent, and of
priests, *vv.* 61–63, who could not trace their priestly
genealogy. These distinctions evidently fit better the
later time of Nehemiah.

[1] P. 34.

To understand the restoration at the close of the
exile it is necessary to gain a true conception of the
state of things in Palestine during the Exile. The
amount of definite information available is very small;
the later Jews were only too anxious to throw a veil
over those distressful years.

King Sargon of Assyria has left us a cuneiform
record of the deportations from Israel at the time of
the fall of Samaria in 722 B.C. He deported 27,290
people, and though this is a considerable deportation
it cannot have left the land by any means denuded.
The writer of II Sam. xxiv. 9 gives the number of
men of military age in Northern Israel in the time of
David as 800,000. In A.D. 1914 the total population
of the whole of Palestine was only about 700,000; but
this figure represents only 15 per cent. (according to
Reclus), or even 10 per cent. (according to Colonel
Conder) of the population which it supported in the
days of its prosperity[1]. Sargon's monument is a contemporary communiqué, and like other communiqués
would be more likely to overestimate than underesti-
mate the extent of the victory. We can take it as an
outside number, and need not take seriously the statement of the moralizing writer of II Kings xvii. 18 that
"Yahweh was very angry with Israel, and removed
them out of His sight: there was none left but the
tribe of Judah only." With regard to the later deportation of Judah, II Kings xxv. 22 admits that they
were not all carried away to Babylon, but verse 26
referring to those that remained says that after the
murder of Gedaliah "all the people, both small and

[1] *Zionism and the Jewish Future*, ed. Sacher, p. 156.

great, and the captains of the forces, arose and came to Egypt." The writer of II Kings therefore supposed that all the Israelites, of both the northern and the southern kingdom, were scattered. Jer. xliii. 5–7 also says that all the remnant of Judah went down to Egypt, but the total number deported to Babylon is given in Jer. lii. 28–30 as 4,600. The writer could scarcely have supposed that a larger number went to Egypt than to Babylon, and therefore it may be taken as certain that a considerable number remained in Judah just as a considerable number had remained in the northern kingdom after the fall of Samaria.

There is a good deal of evidence that after the land of Judah was partially depopulated, tribes from the south immigrated into Judah and intermarried with the Jews. This suggestion is borne out by the fact that in the lists of Israelites preserved in I Chron. there are included the names of tribes that had not of old been regarded as Israelite, *e.g.* Caleb (ii. 9, 18, iv. 15), Jerahmeel (ii. 9, 25), Kenites (ii. 55), Kenaz (iv. 13). Ezek. xvi. 45, 46 indicates such intermarriages. It says, speaking to Judah, "Your mother was a Hittite, and your father an Amorite; and thine elder sister is Samaria, that dwelleth at thy left hand [*i.e.* on the north] she and her daughters; and thy younger sister, that dwelleth at thy right hand [*i.e.* on the south] is Sodom and her daughters." The immigration of Edomites into Judah and Israel is recorded in Ezek. xxxv. 10 and xxxvi. 3–5, and also in I Esdr. iv. 50 which forms part of the original book of Ezra.

In the northern kingdom of Israel the introduction of foreigners was, at any rate partially, carried out by

force by the king of Assyria (II Kings xvii. 24).
According to II Kings xvii. the Samaritans were simply
the descendants of these immigrants, and had no
Israelite blood in them. But it must be remembered
that this is an *ex parte* statement, by an author who
painted all the northerners in the worst possible light,
and whose verdict of every one of the northern kings
was that he did that which was evil in the sight of the
Lord. An important work on the Samaritans was
published at Philadelphia, U.S.A., in 1907[1], in which
the author recounts what is known of the later history
of the Samaritans, and comes to the conclusion that
their origin cannot be explained as described in
II Kings xvii. He says[2], "When at last we come
upon definite information concerning the Samaritans,
of the kind that gives some description of them—and
these authorities belong to the Christian era, the New
Testament, Josephus, the Talmud—the Samaritans
appear as nothing else than a Jewish sect. The one
essential difference between them and Judaism is that
their cult centres on Gerizim, not on Zion." But what
is perhaps more surprising than absence of heathen
connexions, is that no connexion can be traced with
the Israelite calf-worship. We read in Jer. xli. 5 that
soon after the fall of Jerusalem certain men came from
Shechem, Shiloh and Samaria to make an offering in
the (ruined) temple of Jerusalem. This shows that in
those days some at any rate of the people of the
northern province were willing to join the Yahweh worship at Jerusalem. It seems very likely that common

[1] J. A. Montgomery, *The Samaritans.*
[2] *Op. cit.*, p. 46.

cause was made to a great extent between North
and South during the dark days of the Exile. As early
as the reign of Jeroboam II the northern kingdom
had been subject to religious propaganda from Judah
(Amos vii. 10–15). After the fall of Samaria king
Josiah of Judah was able to push his religious reforms
into the northern province, and he destroyed the altar
and high place at Bethel as well as the other high
places in the cities of Samaria (II Kings xxiii. 15–20).
We may well believe that from that time the northerners
did not continue the use of the calf-idol. If so they had
given up the one thing that separated them from the
Jews of Judah and Jerusalem. At any rate, whenever
the *rapprochement* took place, the Jews and the
Samaritans during part of the post-exilic period were
sufficiently at one for both to have in common the
same Book of the Law. "Even as the Samaritans are
shown by anthropology to be Hebrews of the Hebrews,
so the study of their religion and manners demonstrates
them to be nothing else than a Jewish sect. This is not
the traditional view concerning their origin, nor is it as
yet generally known to the lay mind. Samaritanism
is still commonly looked upon as a mixed religion containing elements of Judaism and ancient heathenism[1]."

With the immigration of foreigners into Palestine,
and with the Hebrew national sense weakened by the
loss of kingly power, intermarriage of both Jews and
Samaritans with foreigners must have been pretty
general. The Jews deported to Babylon probably
intermarried less, though it is unlikely that they kept
absolutely distinct. When the Jews began to return to

[1] Montgomery, *op. cit.*, pp. 27, 28.

Judah they spoke of the inhabitants of the land, both
in Judah and in Samaria, as עַם הָאָרֶץ 'the people of
the land,' a title in itself implying no disrespect. When
stress was laid on their foreign blood they were called
עַמֵּי הָאָרֶץ 'peoples of the land,' but when stress was
laid on their Jewish blood they were called הַשְּׁאֵרִית
'the remnant.' The people whom Haggai exhorted to
rebuild the temple are called both 'the remnant' and
'the people of the land.'

CHAPTER IV

THE BUILDING OF THE TEMPLE

UNTIL quite recently there was no knowledge of any Jewish temple outside Palestine, except for the admittedly schismatical temple founded by Onias at Leontopolis in the middle of the second century B.C.

The publication of the Aramaic papyri from Elephantine has given a new insight into the life of the Jews living outside Palestine. Elephantine, or Yeb as it is called in the papyri, is an island at Assouan (Syene) near the first cataract of the Nile. There was a Jewish colony at this place, and they had a temple of their own in which they offered sacrifices to Yahu. The date of the building of the temple is uncertain, but it was certainly standing in the sixth and fifth centuries B.C. In Sachau's papyrus I the Jews state that Cambyses (529–522) did not harm their temple when he invaded Egypt. At first sight it is difficult to reconcile the existence of this temple with the insistence in Deuteronomy on the single sanctuary at Jerusalem. It looks as if the Jews in Egypt at any rate did not consider that the Deuteronomic law of the single sanctuary applied outside Palestine, and it is even possible that the Jews in Palestine held the same view. If so it certainly raises the possibility that Jews scattered in other parts also had temples for the worship of Yahweh. Thus Torrey says, "There were similar religious conditions in other similar colonies, and it may well be that we shall discover, some day, that in Babylonia and elsewhere there were flourishing Jewish temples, in which sacrifice to Yahwè was offered in the time-honored way[1]."

The suggestion was recently made in the *Journal of Theological Studies*[2] that Ezr. viii. 17 contains a reference to such a sanctuary. It was shown that a possible translation of the passage was as follows: "And I (*i.e.* Ezra) sent them to Iddo the chief priest in the sanctuary at Casiphia; and I put in their mouth words to speak unto Iddo my brother and the Nethinim in the sanctuary at Casiphia, to bring unto us servants for the house of our God[3]." This, as we shall see, is from Ezra's Memoirs, and if the translation put forward is correct it would show that there was a temple at the Babylonian town called Casiphia at the end of the fifth century B.C., and that Ezra's brother Iddo was chief priest there. It must have been an important sanctuary, for Iddo had a sufficiently large staff to be able to spare some forty Levites and 220 Nethinim to go to Palestine. That Ezra called the sanctuary by no more honorific title than the colourless word מָקוֹם only reflects his estimate of other sanctuaries compared with the great temple of Jerusalem.

[1] *Ezra Studies*, p. 317.

[2] In a note by the author, "A Jewish Sanctuary in Babylonia," July 1916.

[3] The only emendation of the text necessary for this translation is to alter the word division אֶחָיו הַנְּתוּנִים, which is untranslatable, to אֶחָי וְהַנְּתוּנִים. Examples are adduced of the use of מקום for 'sanctuary' (II Kings v. 11), and of הראש for 'chief priest' (II Chron. xxiv. 6); and 'Casiphia the sanctuary' means 'the sanctuary at Casiphia' as clearly as 'Shushan the castle' means 'the castle at Shushan' (Neh. i. 1, Dan. viii. 2, etc.).

But whatever temples and sanctuaries the Jews may
have had outside Palestine these would not make up
for the absence of a temple at Jerusalem. In fact the
continuance of the ritual of sacrifice in other sanctuaries would be a daily reminder of the once famous
sanctuary of Zion, and Jews returning from abroad
would feel the more acutely the lack of a temple in
their mother city. One would therefore expect that
the restoration of the Jerusalem temple would be
undertaken under the influence, direct or indirect, of
the dispersed Jews. It was the opinion of the Chronicler that the whole work was done by Jews from
Babylon who had returned to Palestine. For instance,
Ezr. iii. 8 (with the conclusion of the sentence added
from the parallel passage I Esdr. v. 54, 55, E.V. v.
56, 57) says, "Now in the second year of their coming
unto the house of God at Jerusalem, in the second
month, began Zerubbabel the son of Shealtiel, and
Jeshua the son of Jozadak, and the rest of their
brethren the priests and Levites, and all they that were
come out of the captivity unto Jerusalem, [and they
laid the foundation of the temple of God on the New
Moon of the second month of the second year of their
coming to Judaea and Jerusalem.]" Ezr. vi. 16 says,
"And the children of Israel, the priests and the Levites,
and the rest of the children of the captivity, kept the
dedication of this house of God with joy"; and vi. 19
says, "And the children of the captivity kept the passover upon the fourteenth day of the first month."
Against the historicity of the Chronicler's narrative
we have already seen[1] that according to Haggai there

---

[1] P. 44.

was no foundation of the temple before the reign of Darius. But Haggai leads us to question even further the Chronicler's story, for according to Hag. ii, 2, 4 it was the 'remnant of the people' or 'the people of the land' whom Haggai exhorted to build, and according to Hag. i. 12, 14 it was actually the 'remnant of the people' who with Zerubbabel and Jeshua laid the foundation of the temple. From this it must be concluded that the actual work was undertaken by the old inhabitants and not by returned exiles. The same is made even clearer by Haggai's appeal to them as men who lived in cieled houses (Hag. i. 4) which could not have been said of people who had just immigrated from Babylon. But two points are worthy of notice: first that the restoration of the temple did not take place till after the Jews in Babylon had been granted freedom to depart; and secondly that Zerubbabel's name, whether it means 'begotten in Babylon' or not, probably has something to do with Babylon. We are inclined to conclude that though the actual work was done by the old inhabitants, the impulse and incentive came from Babylon.

One passage in Hag. (ii. 10–14) has caused a good deal of difficulty, which is removed by a suggestion recently put forward by Rothstein[1]. In this section the question is asked whether holiness can be communicated by touch, and the answer is No; whether uncleanness can be communicated by touch, and the answer is Yes. Then Haggai says that 'this people, this nation' is likewise unclean, and they defile all

[1] J. W. Rothstein, *Juden und Samaritaner*, 1908, in Kittel's *Beiträge z. Wiss. v. AT.*

that they touch. The usual interpretation of this is that the defilement of the temple was communicated to the land and the people of Israel and to all their works, and that for that reason their crops failed (ii. 15–19). But there is a great difficulty in the way of this view. On the twenty-fourth day of the sixth month, in response to Haggai's preaching, the people of Israel had begun to build. On the twenty-first day of the seventh month the work was progressing well, and Yahweh said that He was with them, and that His spirit abode upon them (Hag. ii. 4, 5). And though they were often backsliding, and needed exhortation to repentance some time during the eighth month, yet the path of repentance was still open (Zech. i. 1–4). Is it then conceivable that Yahweh should tell the people on the twenty-fourth day of the ninth month that they were hopelessly unclean? Moreover the form of expression הָעָם הַזֶּה הַגּוֹי הַזֶּה, 'this people, this nation,' is extremely contemptuous. These reasons led Rothstein to see that the nation referred to could not be the people of Israel, but that they were the Samaritans. The current interpretation of the passage is of course conditioned by the following verses 15–19, which refer to the failure of the Israelites to build the temple; and if verses 10–14 do not refer to Israelites they cannot originally have been immediately followed by verses 15–19. As a matter of fact internal evidence of ii. 15–19 shows conclusively that this section did not originally stand in its present position. The Jews were asked to compare their past and the unfruitfulness of their land with what it would be in the future, and the day on which the change of Yahweh's favour was to take place was the day on which the prophet spoke—"from this day and onwards," verse 15. The day is further defined in the same verse as "from before the laying of one stone upon another in the temple of the Lord." Thus the day on which the prophet spoke was before the actual building had begun, and this shows that the section is not in its original chronological position. Rothstein thinks that this speech was made on the actual day of the foundation stone laying, and that is possible if Haggai was speaking before the ceremony of the laying of the stone. But the speech may just as easily have been made shortly before that day, as far as the internal evidence of the section goes. It is true that verse 18 says that the date was the day of the foundation stone laying, but the value of that statement is discounted by the fact that the date given there (ninth month, twenty-fourth day) does not tally with the date given in i. 15 (sixth month, twenty-fourth day). But it is evident that Haggai in his speech had no need to mention the date, and the date is therefore generally agreed to be a later insertion. The reason why a wrong date for the foundation was inserted is of minor importance. The easiest supposition is that a glossator added the date of the foundation stone laying (sixth month, twenty-fourth day) together with the words "since the day that the foundation of the Lord's temple was laid" while the section was in its true position. Contrast the perfect tense of the verb in the sentence just quoted (לְמִן־הַיּוֹם אֲשֶׁר־יֻסַּד הֵיכַל־יהוה) with the timeless infinitive in

verse 15 (מְטֶּרֶם שׂוּם־אֶבֶן אֶל־אֶבֶן בְּהֵיכַל־יהוה). Then
after the section had been accidentally moved to its
present position the date was altered to the ninth
month to agree with ii. 10. This is perhaps rather
easier than supposing that the wrong date was inserted in the first case by the glossator. Rothstein[1],
in trying to find the original position of ii. 15-19,
suggests the end of chapter i. But there are three
objections to this position. In the first place it would
bring the speech after the ceremony of foundation
laying, which would seem to be precluded by the
words "from before the laying of one stone upon
another." Secondly, chapter i. ends, not with a speech
but with a piece of history, and if the speech were inserted here it would lack an introduction. Thirdly, it
would be too late to hope for any change in the pros-
pects for fruit harvest (ii. 19), as the harvest would be
almost over. Verse 19 with its rather obscure question
about the grain deserves some consideration. It runs,
"Is the seed yet[2] in the barn? Moreover the vine and
the fig tree and the pomegranate and the olive tree
have not brought forth. From this day will I bless
you." As we have seen that the section belongs to
the sixth month and not to the ninth it cannot mean
that the seed was already sown, for that would not
take place till October (seventh–eighth month). The
sort of answer probably expected was, "The harvest
of grain was so small that in the two or three months
since harvest the supply has been rapidly used up,

[1] *Op. cit.*, p. 63.
[2] Has Mitchell (*ad loc.*) any authority for translating עוֹד 'already'?

and we are always in doubt whether we shall find any
in the barn either for food or for the coming sowing."
At the moment of speaking the fruit trees had not
borne fruit. There is an evident distinction between
the grain, the harvest of which had been very poor,
and the fruit trees which had not yet borne ripe fruit.
This could not easily be the case on the twenty-fourth
day of the sixth month (where Rothstein would place
it), for by that time the figs and grapes would be ripe
and the olives ripening, though it is only fair to him
to say that he is inclined to think that verse 19*a* is a
later addition. But why should not ii. 15–19 be the
original conclusion to Haggai's speech after i. 11?
Budde had already noticed that verse 11 was an
abrupt ending to a sermon[1]. That sermon was delivered on the first day of the sixth month, which would
fit in well with the condition of the fruits, for at
that date (somewhere between August 1st and Sep-
tember 1st) the particular kind of fig mentioned
(תְּאֵנָה) would ordinarily be beginning to ripen in the
neighbourhood of Jerusalem, while the olive and grape
would not be ripe. Moreover the section ii. 15–19
carries on exactly the thought of i. 6–11. Haggai exhorted them to build by promising them that from that
day Yahweh would bless them (ii. 19) if they repented.

---

[1] *Z. at. W.* XXVI (1906), Karl Budde, "Zum Text d. drei letzten
kleinen Propheten." On Hag. i. 11 he says, "Mit *v.* 11 bricht die Rede
auffallend plötzlich ab. Man muss unbedingt erwarten, dass Haggai auf
die Erklärung der ungünstigen Vergangenheit und Gegenwart noch
einmal eine nachdrückliche Mahnung zum Tempelbau und die Verheis-
sung einer besseren Zukunft hat folgen lassen....Fragen kann man nur
ob schon der erste Berichterstatter Haggais Rede so zusammengezogen
hat, oder ob erst nachher hinter *v.* 11 der Abschluss verloren gegangen
ist. Das letztere ist das wahrscheinlichere."

The story then goes on (Hag. i. 12) to say how
Zerubbabel and Joshua and all the remnant of the
people obeyed and feared, and with further exhortation from Haggai they came and began the work
on the twenty-fourth day of the sixth month. About
a month later (the twenty-first day of the seventh
month, Hag. ii. 1) Haggai comforted the old people
who had seen the former temple and were disap-
pointed in the meaner dimensions of the new house.
Haggai's method of comforting them is rather remarkable: he says that Yahweh will bring about a world-
catastrophe (ii. 6, "I will shake the heavens and the
earth and the sea and the dry land"), and that as a result all the treasures of the nations shall be brought to
beautify the house. In Deutero-Isaiah the renewed
prosperity of Israel was due to Yahweh's favour, but
was conditioned by the behaviour of Israel and the
fact that Israel was already overpunished. The means
of restored prosperity was through the workings of history and particularly through Cyrus. Here in Haggai
we have suddenly stepped out into the realm of apocalyptic: without any warrant in the contemporary
historical events Haggai looked forward to a miraculous intervention of Yahweh whereby the magni-
ficence of His house would be assured. Deutero-
Isaiah had been optimistic about things as he saw
them, believing that they would develop under the
guiding hand of God to better things; but Haggai,
like all apocalyptists, was pessimistic about the present
world order—the only hope was for Yahweh to shake
the universe like a dice-box and throw the dice again.

Before going further with Haggai's story let us turn

to Ezr. iv. 1–3. The narrative there tells of an offer on the part of "the adversaries of Judah and Benjamin" to assist in the building of the temple. As the text stands this refers to the supposed building in the days of Cyrus, which we have seen reason to dispute. But it is quite possible that the section contains an element of true history, viz. that an offer of help was made, only that it was in the reign of Darius. The people who made the offer are clearly intended to be the Samaritans by the story of their origin; but the wording is equally clearly not theirs, for they would not have denied their Israelite origin, nor would they, or any contemporary for that matter, have described the Samaritans as early as this as the enemies of Judah and Benjamin. Verse 3 relates that Zerubbabel and Jeshua and the rest of the heads of families of Israel refused the proffered help, alleging as a reason that such help was excluded by the terms of Cyrus' decree.

Now turn back to Hag. ii. 10–14 and read how and why this refusal was really made. It was Haggai himself, or perhaps the priests, who were responsible. They said that uncleanness was catching, and that the Samaritans—'this people, this nation,' as they are contemptuously called—were unclean and would defile the temple by working at it and by the gifts which they would offer when the temple was built. It was true enough that, according to the recognized ritual, uncleanness could be communicated by touch; but it was mere assumption that the Samaritans were unclean. One can only conjecture the reason for this assumption, but it may well be that some spark of the old tribal jealousy between the North and South

Kingdoms had survived through all the political changes, and that the inhabitants of Judah did not love their northern neighbours. There seems to be no suggestion at this stage of objection to the Samaritans on the ground of mixed marriages with non-Jews. The builders of the temple were probably of mixed stock equally with the Samaritans, and it was not till the time of Nehemiah and Ezra that the attempt was made to separate a purely Jewish stock. It may be asked whether there is any foundation for the excuse given in Ezr. iv. 3 that Samaritan help was excluded by the terms of the decree of Cyrus. The answer probably is that that was the excuse which was allowed to reach the Persian Court.

The policy of refusing the Samaritan help was a dangerous one. In the first place the help was badly needed, and its absence would make the work much more difficult, and in the second place it was dangerous to provoke the enmity of an important neighbour. Jeshua did not need any persuasion, as he was of the priestly caste who had started the plot ("Ask now the priests..." Hag. ii. 11), but Zerubbabel needed encouragement, and Haggai gave this (ii. 20-23) as before by an apocalyptic promise of a catastrophe in which all the enemies of Judah would be miraculously overthrown, with the added lure that Zerubbabel himself should be the Servant of Yahweh to perform His will, and the Chosen of Yahweh, i.e. the leader of Yahweh's triumphant hosts.

The feelings of the Samaritans in being rejected in this way from the worship of Israel must have been rather mixed: the more religious would feel keenly the religious loss, while the less religious would be incensed by the political insult. The attitude of the latter section is reflected in Ezr. iv. 4, 5, but rather blurred in the process of reflection. There is reason to think that these two verses are not by the same hand as verses 1–3: the characters in the early verses are the "adversaries of Judah and Benjamin" and "the children of the captivity," but in the later verses they are "the people of the land" and "the people of Judah." It is difficult to think of open schism as early as this between the Samaritans and the Jews, because of the reception of the Pentateuch by the Samaritans at a later time. On the other hand it is easy to understand why the Chronicler should have set these verses 4, 5 in this place, for they give an explanation of the long interval supposed by the Chronicler between the foundation stone laying and the actual building. Like the other elaborations of the Chronicler, these verses were probably founded on fact, and the one thing that is likely to be a fact is that the Samaritans "hired counsellors against the Jews." The reason for thinking that this was a fact is that chapters v. and vi. record an enquiry into the building of the temple instituted by Tattenai the Persian "Governor beyond the River." The Aramaic letter of Tattenai, which the Chronicler was using[1], was earlier than the Chronicler, and is probably based on fact. The interesting thing is that although Tattenai instituted this enquiry he does not seem to have stopped the work pending the decision. This suggests that he himself was not unfavourably disposed towards the Jews, but that he had been

[1] See p. 41.

persuaded to make the enquiry by the allegations of certain men. These men would of course be the counsellors hired by the Samaritans to frustrate the work. It is easy to imagine this sort of underground intrigue going on, fostered by certain Samaritan leaders, without the whole Samaritan community having made a breach with the Jews.

The intrigue failed. Darius permitted the work to go on, and cited a decree of Cyrus granting the permission. We need not trouble about the wording of the decree as given, which differs so greatly from the version in Ezr. i. It is sufficient to know that in some form or other Cyrus had granted the permission. And that we do know as a fact from his policy as declared on his Cylinder: "All gods, which I have returned to their towns, shall daily proclaim before Bel and Nebo the length of my days."

We have a further piece of evidence which points to a fear on the part of the Jews of an attack on Jerusalem. Zech. ii. 5–9 (E.V. 1–5) indicates that some of the Jews were desirous of building the city walls. The prophet in his vision saw a young man about to measure the breadth and length of Jerusalem, and the prophet was bidden to go and say to him, "Jerusalem shall sit as open regions, by reason of the multitude of men and cattle therein. For I, saith the Lord, will be unto her a wall of fire round about, and I will be glory in the midst of her." As far as the words go this vision might be supposed to mean that the Jews were anxious for the increase of the population of the city. But though that question became important later (Neh. vii. 4, xi. 1) it was only of importance after the walls had been built. Rothstein must surely be correct[1] in interpreting this vision as the indication of a policy to build the walls. The young man was measuring lengths, not counting the population, and Yahweh's answer was that greatly populated as the city would become it would be open like hamlets because Yahweh would be a wall of protection round about. Whether the Samaritans ever got actually so far as to plan an attack on Jerusalem may be questioned, but some of the Jews may well have feared such a possibility and have suggested the building of the walls as a desirable precaution. Zechariah with greater foresight refused to build the walls, knowing that such an action would only support any accusations of disloyalty which the Samaritans might make to the Persian authorities.

The attitude of Haggai and Zechariah to the building of the temple was rather different. Haggai looked on it as a duty of Israel which was a necessary condition before they could expect Yahweh's favour (Hag. i. 9, ii. 15–19). Zechariah was also very desirous of seeing the temple rebuilt; note the eagerness with which he exhorted Zerubbabel to overcome all difficulties in the way of the restoration (Zech. iv. 6–10a), but to him the restoration of the temple was itself the sign of Yahweh's returning favour—"I am returning to Jerusalem with mercies; my house shall be built in it, saith Yahweh Sabaoth" (Zech. i. 16). As far as our records go Haggai's sole interest was in the restoration of the sanctuary. Zechariah realized that that was not the only nor the most pressing need of the Jews, and

---

[1] *Die Nachtgesichte des Sacharja*, pp. 78–81.

he laid great stress on social virtues (Zech. vii. 9, 10, viii. 16, 17).

Allusion has already been made to the apocalyptic outlook of Haggai. Zechariah's outlook was of the same character; and as their teaching and run of ideas were dependent on their expectations for the future, these expectations are deserving of some consideration. The most surprising thing for anyone who has followed the prophecies of Deutero-Isaiah is to find Zerubbabel addressed as the Servant of the Lord. Haggai said, "In that day, saith Yahweh Sabaoth, I will take thee, O Zerubbabel, my Servant, the son of Shealtiel, saith Yahweh, and will make thee as a signet; for I have chosen thee, saith Yahweh Sabaoth" (Hag. ii. 23). Zechariah addressed him with the title of Servant and also the title of 'Branch' by which Jeremiah had designated the Messianic king of David's line (Jer. xxiii. 5, xxxiii. 15), "For behold I will bring forth my Servant the Branch" (Zech. iii. 8), "Behold the man, whose name is the Branch; and he shall grow up out of his place, and he shall build the temple of Yahweh" (Zech. vi. 12). That Zerubbabel is intended, though not mentioned explicitly by name, is clear from the reference to the builder of the temple, cf. Zech. iv. 9, "The hands of Zerubbabel have laid the foundations of this house; his hands shall also finish it." Different as Zerubbabel was from the Servant of Yahweh as depicted by Deutero-Isaiah, the use of the term shows that Haggai and Zechariah had some acquaintance with Deutero-Isaiah's prophecy, even if they did not enter into the true spirit of it. For Deutero-Isaiah the Servant of Yahweh denoted Israel as commissioned to carry out Yahweh's

will for Israel and for the gentile world. Now Haggai
and Zechariah thought that Zerubbabel was leading
Israel to fulfil this task. For Haggai and Zechariah, and
especially for the former, the first part of the restoration
of Israel was the rejection of the Samaritans. That
Zerubbabel was already doing. The fact that Zerubbabel had no missionary zeal for the gentiles did not
trouble Haggai, because he believed that the gentiles
would be brought in miraculously by the sudden intervention of Yahweh (Hag. ii. 7). Zechariah more explicitly declares the future inclusion of the gentiles,
"Many nations shall join themselves to the Lord in that
day, and shall be my people" (Zech. ii. 15, E.V. 11).
But he conceived this as happening only on the day,
the great day, of the Lord's intervention, as he makes
clearer in iii. 9, "I will remove the iniquity of that land *in
one day*"—no ordinary process of betterment, but the
power of the arm of the Lord. Important in this connexion is the vision of the four chariots and horses
sent forth, apparently, to the four quarters of the earth
(Zech. vi. 1–8). The vision is hard of interpretation.
For what purpose did the horses go forth? R.V. by its
translation "have quieted my spirit," *i.e.* "have appeased
my wrath," and Mitchell, think it was to take vengeance
on the heathen. But this is not what one would expect
after the hope in ii. 15 (E.V. ii. 11) that the gentiles
should become the people of God. Rothstein thinks
it was to bring in the scattered Israelites—but this
would then be out of context, for the previous visions
had already spoken about the future Jerusalem and
the coming of the Messianic Age. All that was required
now was to deal with the heathen. And the one

5—2

purpose which satisfies the context is that the horses
and chariots went out to convert the heathen: the four
winds or spirits of God went forth, and there especially
in the dark north country (Babylon, by the way, was
thought of as being north) the Spirit of God was to be
given rest, "Behold, they that go toward the north
country have caused my spirit to rest in the north
country" (Zech. vi. 8). Even in the heathen country
to which Wickedness had been banished (Zech. v. 11)
Yahweh's Spirit was to find rest. But in all this
Zechariah had no missionary ideas. The inclusion of
the gentiles was to be the work of Yahweh in the great
day. If gentiles are referred to in vi. 15, "they that
are far off shall come and build in the temple of the
Lord," it doubtless only means after their conversion
when they have become Jews; but the verse may
equally well refer to scattered Israelites.

An interesting question arises whether Zechariah
supported Haggai's policy of rejecting the Samaritans.
An affirmative answer is suggested by a rather attrac-
tive interpretation of the vision, iii. 1-7, of Joshua
arrayed in filthy garments and accused by the Satan.
This accusation in heaven by the Satan represents or
corresponds to an earthly accusation against Joshua.
The question is, Who accused Joshua, and what was he
accused of? Ewald thought that he was attacked, or
threatened with attack, by the Persian Court, but this
is unlikely for any political attack would be directed
against Zerubbabel the political head of Judaea. Many
commentators have thought that the reference was not
to Joshua's personal guilt, but to the guilt of the whole
people, but that idea can only be got from verse 9

which does not really belong to the vision. Now we have seen that the decision to reject the Samaritans was taken by Haggai at the instigation of the priests, and we read in Ezr. iv. 3 that Zerubbabel was supported by Joshua the High Priest when he conveyed this decision to the people. We may therefore conclude that if Joshua had any enemies they were among the rejected Samaritans and their friends. If they wanted to lay an accusation against Joshua the easiest thing to say was an *et tu quoque*. The priests had said that the Samaritans were unclean (Hag. ii. 14), so Joshua is accused of being unclean, and is pictured as arrayed in filthy garments (Zech. iii. 3). This accusation was no doubt based on the fact that Joshua had come from Babylon, where the Jews must have mingled with the heathen to a great extent. The image was perhaps suggested by Jeremiah's linen girdle which was marred by being left near the Euphrates, Jer. xiii. 1–11. Yahweh's answer was to the effect that Joshua by returning from Babylon had been saved from Babylon's uncleanness, he was a "brand plucked out of the fire[1]." If this is the correct interpretation of the vision it puts Zechariah on the side of Joshua and the priests, and shows that he supported them in their anti-Samaritan policy.

[1] This expression is borrowed from Amos iv. 11, where it was reminiscent of the rescue of Lot from Sodom and Gomorrah.

CHAPTER V

THE REJECTED SAMARITANS

SOME of the later chapters of Isaiah have the charm of unsolved riddles. They invite the adventurer to try new paths to see if they lead anywhere. Some of our ablest scholars have, as a matter of fact, studied these chapters; and one would hesitate greatly before proposing any new theories, but for one fact—that all these authorities have reached different conclusions. The great divergences of opinion as to the dates and occasions of the later chapters of Isaiah suggest that the truth has not yet been discovered. That is the excuse for the new interpretation now offered.

I. *The Plaint of a Samaritan Prophet.*

The first and crucial section to be considered is Is. lxiii. 7–lxiv. 11. It is a section which stands out clearly from what precedes and from what follows, and is pretty clearly a unity in itself. Even those commentators who would divide it into paragraphs are not in agreement. The unity of the whole section will be made the more apparent as we go on. For the present we will assume it, and leave till later Marti's suggestion that lxiv. 9–11 (E.V. 10–12) is a later addition.

It is perhaps not very surprising that no commentator has found a really suitable occasion for this prophecy. The great gaps in Jewish history, which we can only fill in by our imagination, would be sufficient to account for sections without a context. Yet it must be admitted that the modern tendency is rather dangerous which relegates all our 'orphan' sections to the gaps where the commentator is at liberty to write his own history with no evidence to contradict him. But even if we can find no context for the prophecy as a whole, we might at least expect it to be intelligible. As at present interpreted it is not even intelligible: several verses, where there is no suspicion of textual corruption, have simply baffled the commentators. Undoubtedly the most difficult of these baffling phrases is lxiii. 16, "For thou art our Father, for Abraham knoweth us not, and Israel doth not acknowledge us; thou, O Yahweh, art our Father; our Redeemer from everlasting is thy name." The majority of commentators seem to take the words 'know' and 'acknowledge' in the sense of 'help' or 'succour,' and see a contrast between the patriarchs who do not help their descendants, and Yahweh, the true father, who does help; for instance, Rosenmüller, "Tu iustius pater noster diceris, quam illi, ex quibus naturae ordine geniti sumus, et qui nos in his malis constitutos sublevare non possunt." Only Calvin apparently preserved the ungarnished meaning of 'knowing.' He took the argument to be similar to that of xlix. 15, "Can a woman forget her sucking child, that she should not have compassion on the son of her womb? yea, these may forget, yet will not I forget thee." Calvin says, "potius enim naturae jura cessabunt, quam te nobis patrem non praebeas." The difficulty in this interpretation is the meaning that has to be put into כִּי as if it meant 'though[1].' Calvin's interpretation may therefore be dismissed, and we are thrown back upon the mass of commentators who think that the prophet is asserting that Abraham and Israel do not *help* their descendants. Immediately two questions arise, Why should the prophet allude at all to the fact that no help was forthcoming from the patriarchs? and did he mean that they could not or that they would not help? These questions of course should never have arisen; they only result from giving the words יָדַע and יַכִּיר a meaning which they do not contain. Commentators have bravely faced the difficulties in which they found themselves. Thus Cheyne says[2], "Is it not a platitude to say that the remote ancestors of the Jews cannot help them, unless there was some chance from the popular point of view (and obs., the prophet is speaking in the name of the people), that they might both sympathise and powerfully co-operate with their descendants—unless, in short, they were regarded somewhat as demi-gods (comp. the Homeric poems), or patron saints, or the angelic 'holy ones' in a speech of Eliphaz the Temanite (Job v. 1)?" Duhm's comment (*ad loc.*) is as follows, "We have no other father; Abraham, Israel (the founder of our race) know us not. If this sentence is not mere phraseology, it must have seemed possible to many contemporaries to get help from ancestors (even if not exactly from Abraham or Jacob). That need not have been real ancestor-

---

[1] Cheyne, *Prophecies of Isaiah*, Vol. II, 2nd ed. 1882, p. 299, says "Is כִּי ever 'though,' unless perhaps when its clause stands first?"

[2] *Op. cit.*, p. 107.

worship; there is also the possibility that it was necromancy." Marti (*ad loc.*) observes, "The argument puts the patriarchs and Yahweh, the true father of Israel, in opposition. Many of the author's contemporaries expected help from the former, apparently because they regarded these ancestors as semi-divine beings and venerated (verehrten) them as such." It will be observed that these authors assume for their argument the existence of ancestor-worship or something very much like it among the Israelites. It is true that some authorities believe that ancestor-worship played a part in the religious development of Israel, but others equally strongly deny it. The evidence for it is certainly not overwhelming, and if it did exist the times when it would be most likely to be practised would be in the pre-Mosaic days, or at latest in the monolatrous days, and certainly not at this late hour when the prophetical monotheism had won the field. "It is worth noticing that despite the fact that nearly every advanced critic declares that the ancestors of the nations were gods to whom divine honours were paid at the ancient sanctuaries, there are few traces of anything of the kind in the Bible. If it is suggested that this was deliberately cut out by the revisers of the records of Israel after the Return, why, I ask, should they not have omitted all allusion to high-place worship, human sacrifice, ritual impurity, and a great many more things which are frankly acknowledged? The obvious inference is that no such thing entered the mind of the ordinary Israelite, and that he never dreamed of deifying Abraham, Jacob, or even Moses. To him, as to us, they were simply great men to whom God had revealed His will[1]." It cannot of course be denied that there may have been individuals in Israel who were ready to seek help in difficulties from the spirits of the deceased, but the use of such 'black arts' is always anti-social, that is, they are employed by the individual to promote his individual ends, as in the case of Saul and the witch of En-dor, or in the cases of present-day animistic peoples, when those ends conflict with what is for the good of the community as a whole. That is why magic and necromancy are always looked down on in any respectable community. In any national or tribal trouble the source from which help would naturally be sought is the national or tribal deity; and it is scarcely conceivable that the people of Israel, or a section of the people, expected or sought help from spirits of the deceased, instead of from Yahweh, in their national distress, especially when one of the things they were praying for was the restoration of the temple of Yahweh. The difficulty is increased when one asks whether the prophet himself shared the view of the people that the patriarchs could help but would not do so. Cheyne supposed that the prophet was not simply condescending to the popular phraseology, but actually endorsed the words which he uttered in the name of the people. That is, Cheyne supposed that the prophet ascribed the inattention of the patriarchs not to their inability to help but to the degeneracy of their descendants. But if the prophet held such a view and yet expected attention from Yahweh it was tantamount to saying that Yahweh

[1] Foakes-Jackson, "The Religion of Northern Israel under the Monarchy," *The Interpreter*, October 1912.

would not take the degeneracy of the people so
seriously as did the patriarchs. Such a view could not
come from a prophet who had any high ideas of
Yahweh, and we must therefore turn to the alternative
view of Goldziher[1] and Duhm[2] that the prophet did
not himself hold the popular opinion that the spirits
of the deceased could help if they wished to do so.
Even then the attitude of the prophet is hard to understand. Had he been addressing the people he might
well have said, "You see that your ancestors have
shown no interest in you, therefore turn and pray to
Yahweh"; but he is addressing God, not the people,
and if he said to God, "We tried Abraham and Jacob
first, but as they failed us we have come to thee, O
Lord" it would not only be an insult to the Deity, but
it would implicate the prophet himself in the unfaith-
fulness of the people.

The impasse to which the current interpretations of
lxiii. 16 have led us, is not the only difficulty. The
words "thy holy cities" עָרֵי קָדְשֶׁךָ in lxiv. 9 (E.V. lxiv.

---

[1] *Mythology among the Hebrews*, trans. by Martineau, 1887. Pages
229 f. "It is obvious that here the names of Abraham and Jacob are
opposed to that of Jahveh. Therefore it is Jahveh, not Abraham;
Jahveh, not Jacob! Jahveh is the omnipotent redeemer and protector
of the people Israel; the others take no care of it. Can we read in this
opposition of names anything else but that the writer wishes to contrast
the idea of a God recognised as the only true with the memory of something different, which ages ago passed for divine, but is unworthy of
adoration now, when the Prophet brings forward the *omniscience* of
Jahveh as an irrefragable argument for the exclusiveness of his divinity?
I think not."

[2] *Ad loc.*, "Our author of course will not hear of it (will nichts davon
wissen), probably not because ancestor-faith has become weaker in his
time, but because it has become stronger and more dangerous."

10) are not yet explained; Cheyne says, "The phrase
is remarkable; elsewhere Jerusalem is 'the holy city.'"
Again it is remarkable in lxiii. 17, to find the people
laying the blame on Yahweh for causing them to err
from His ways; what sort of prophet dared to say
this? or what circumstances could have been sufficient
to provoke the people to such a statement? The translation of lxiii. 19 has caused difficulty: A.V. has, "We
are *thine*: thou never barest rule over them; they were
not called by thy name." R.V. has, "We are become
as they over whom thou never barest rule; as they that
were not called by thy name." The A.V. adds the
word 'thine,' and the R.V. twice adds the word 'as,'
and the meaning provided depends in each case upon
these added words. Yet another difficulty, small perhaps at first sight, but really significant, is the use of
the plural 'tribes of thine inheritance' שִׁבְטֵי נַחֲלָתֶךָ
in lxiii. 17. In the eyes of a Jew what claim had any
tribe but Judah upon the mercy of God?

Those are some of the internal difficulties of the
passage. Before passing on to the new interpretation
which is intended to solve them, it will be well to see
what present-day criticism says as to the occasion of
the prophecy.

Duhm places the prophecy shortly before the visit
of Nehemiah to Jerusalem in 444, and he equates the
desolation mentioned in this chapter with that mentioned in Neh. i. 3. He says (*ad loc.*), "Is. lxiii. 18*b*
refers in all probability to the incident which resulted
in the condition of affairs depicted in Neh. i. 3. 'Our
adversaries' are the Samaritans, they have 'trodden

down thy sanctuary.' Whether מקדש is merely the
temple or the holy city as well is uncertain. In either
case the meaning is much the same; for if the Samaritans trod down the walls of Jerusalem, they also entered
the temple and in the opinion of the Gola they vio-
lated and desecrated it." But Neh. i. 3 says nothing
about the temple being burnt (Is. lxiv. 10, E.V. lxiv.
11) or trampled on (lxiii. 18), and it is quite uncritical
of Duhm to fail to distinguish between the temple and
the walls. A century and a half earlier Jeremiah had
taught the people, effectively one would have supposed,
the folly of pointing to walls and houses and saying,
"The temple of Yahweh, the temple of Yahweh, the
temple of Yahweh, are these" (Jer. vii. 4). The stories
of Zerubbabel building the temple and Nehemiah building the walls show clearly that the two were regarded
as quite distinct. (The distinction was still preserved
in later days, Ben Sira xlix. 11-13.) The assumption
that the adversaries were the Samaritans is un-
warranted, and, as said already, the religious schism
cannot have come before they received the Pentateuch.

Cheyne dated the section a century later than Duhm,
in the reign of Artaxerxes Ochus (358–337), when he
supposed that Jerusalem was attacked and the temple
destroyed. A discussion of the evidence for these events
is given later[1].

Marti resorts to the scissors. lxiv. 9–11 (E.V. 10–12)
he would assign at the earliest to the persecution of
Antiochus Epiphanes, and all the rest he would date
with Duhm in the middle of the fifth century. But the

[1] Pp. 202 ff.

process by which he arrives at this division deserves to be recorded before any weight is laid upon his judgment. It is evident to all commentators that lxiii. 18 *a* is corrupt as it stands in M.T. Gesenius-Buhl suggested as an emendation לָמָּה צָעֲדוּ רְשָׁעִים קָדְשֶׁךָ "Why do the ungodly march over thy Holy Place?" which affords a fitting parallelism to the following words, "our adversaries have trodden down thy sanctuary." Marti accepts this emendation except that he prefers צָעֲרוּ, making it "Why do the ungodly despise thy Holy Place?" Then in the second half of the verse he avoids the word indicating treading on the ruins of the temple by taking בּוֹסְסוּ metaphorically as 'desecrate' instead of in its literal meaning 'tread down.' So translated he regards the verse as evidence that the temple was standing, and it is because lxiv. 9, 10 (E.V. 10, 11) contradict it that he regards the last three verses of the chapter as of a different date. Apart from the discrepancy between lxiii. 18 as emended by Marti and lxiv. 9, 10, there is no evidence whatever for a difference of date, and commentators have generally been struck with the unity of the whole passage.

One thing has already been made clear, that at the time when the prophecy was written the temple was in ruins. This is explicitly stated in lxiii. 18 *b*, and in 18 *a* if Gesenius-Buhl's emendation is correct; and again it is stated explicitly in lxiv. 9, 10 (E.V. 10, 11). The obvious date of the prophecy is just before the restoration of the temple, when the restoration was under discussion. From what has been said in the last chapter about the part the Samaritans wished to play in the restoration it will not be surprising to find in this section the plaint of a Samaritan prophet. Such a thought would have been impossible so long as the Samaritans were regarded as semi-heathen, but now that we know they were Israelites and Yahweh-worshippers it need not surprise us to find a Samaritan prophecy containing some of the highest conceptions of the Deity, a prophecy of such beauty that it has been characterized by Duhm as "ohne Zweifel das Beste, was Tritojesaja geschrieben hat." It was suggested in the last chapter that the religious-minded Samaritans must have felt keenly the refusal of their help in restoring the temple of Yahweh at Jerusalem. Here we have, it seems, the very words of a Samaritan prophet expressing their bitter disappointment at being excluded from the great sanctuary. Had it not been the sin of Jeroboam and his successors that they had refused to worship at Jerusalem? and had not the Israelites in Samaria tried to emend in this matter ever since the fall of the Northern Kingdom? Had they not abolished the calf-worship at Bethel in accordance with the teaching of the prophets? Had not Ezekiel promised them a share in the temple, saying, "And I will set my sanctuary in the midst of them for evermore; and my tabernacle shall be with them"? (Ezek. xxxvii. 26–28). Now they were willing to show in a practical way their devotion to the central sanctuary at Jerusalem by giving their labour to the building, and they had been turned away and told that they had no portion nor inheritance in Israel. The piety, as well as the wisdom, of the prophet is seen in this, that still desiring to be allowed to share

in the temple, he uttered no unkind word about the
party spirit of the men of Judah which had resulted
in the refusal of Samaritan help.   It is in the hope
that the breach may yet be healed that he laid the
blame, not on one section of the nation of Israel,
but on the nation as a whole.   This had been the
character of the people from ancient times: continually
sinning and rebelling in spite of the tender mercies of
Yahweh.

The prophecy begins (lxiii. 7) by recalling the ancient
history of Israel, and the great things that Yahweh had
done for them.   He declared that they were His people,
children who would not deal falsely (יְשַׁקֵּרוּ), v. 8.   The
reference is probably to the confidence in Israel which
led Yahweh to enter into the covenant of Sinai, for the
verb 'to deal falsely' is specially used of covenant-
breaking: cf. Ps. xliv. 18 (E.V. 17) וְלֹא שִׁקַּרְנוּ בִּבְרִיתֶךָ
"neither have we dealt falsely in thy covenant" and
Ps. lxxxix. 34 וְלֹא אֲשַׁקֵּר בֶּאֱמוּנָתִי : לֹא אֲחַלֵּל בְּרִיתִי
"And I will not deal falsely with my faithfulness.
I will not break my covenant."   Verses 8, 9, following
the consonantal text and the Greek version, continue,
"And He became to them a Saviour in all their affliction. Not an ambassador nor a messenger, but His
Presence saved them. In His love and in His pity He
redeemed them."   This refers to the redemption from
Egypt.   Then it goes on, "And He bare them and
carried them all the days of yore," referring to the
carrying through the wilderness as described in Ex.
xix. 4, "Ye have seen what I did to the Egyptians,
and how I bare you on eagles' wings and brought

you unto myself." Verse 10 relates how in spite of this the Israelites rebelled against the Lord: "But they rebelled and grieved His Holy Spirit, therefore He was turned to be their enemy, and Himself fought against them." This is like a summary of Deut. xxxii. 15–25, and probably refers to the rebellions in the wilderness. The first stichos of verse 11 is corrupt, and perhaps a section has dropped out altogether. It reads וַיִּזְכֹּר יְמֵי

עוֹלָם מֹשֶׁה עַמּוֹ "and he remembered the days of old, Moses his people." The Greek has simply καὶ ἐμνή-σθη ἡμερῶν αἰωνίων and omits the rest. Comparing Deut. xxxii. 7 זְכֹר יְמוֹת עוֹלָם "remember the days of old" and its context, it seems likely that 'he remembered' in our passage refers to Israel's recollection and not God's. It may be conjectured that originally there was a short statement of the repentance of the Israel-ites when they considered the days of old, followed by a statement of God's renewed favour. At any rate the verses that follow, beginning "Where is he that brought them up out of the sea?" are not the words of Moses or of the Israelites in the wilderness, for they speak repeatedly of the Israelites in the third person. They are the words of the writer asking for God's interven-tion now in present troubles as He had done of old. At the end of his rhetorical questions the writer turns and addresses God, *v.* 14, "Thus Thou leddest Thy people to make Thyself a glorious name. Look down from heaven and behold, from the high dwelling of Thy holiness and of Thy glory. Where are Thy zeal and Thy mighty acts? Restrain not the yearning of Thy bowels and Thy tender mercies" (reading אַל תִּתְאַפָּק with Oort instead of אֵלַי הִתְאַפָּקוּ). Then (lxiii. 16), in one verse of infinite pathos, the prophet speaks his whole burden of woe, "For Thou art our Father, for Abraham knoweth us not, and Israel doth not acknowledge us; Thou Yahweh art our Father, our Redeemer from everlasting is Thy name." Abraham, the great ancestor from whom the Samaritans were descended, will not know his children. Israel, whose name they had borne *par excellence* from Jeroboam to Hoshea while the Southern Kingdom was called 'the Kingdom of Judah,' would no longer acknowledge them. It was of course not directly, through any necromancy, that the patriarchs had declared the Samaritans outcast, but through the mouth of their descendants the Jews of Jerusalem and Judah. The name of Abraham, like that of Israel, was used not only for the one ancestor of the Hebrews (Ezek. xxxiii. 24, Is. li. 2) but also for the representative of the race (Micah vii. 20). But though thus cast out from Israel the Samaritans yet plead with Yahweh whom they still regard as their Father[1], who had indeed from of old been known as their Redeemer. Their feelings were much like those of David when he said, "They have driven me out this day from joining myself with the inheritance of Yahweh," I Sam. xxvi. 19. Or they felt that they were reversing the sinful judgment of their forefathers who had said, "What portion have we in David? neither have we inheritance in the son of

[1] Cf. Jer. xxxi. 9 "for I am a father to Israel, and Ephraim is my firstborn."

Jesse," I Kings xii. 16. It seemed to the Samaritans that they, the "Ten Tribes," were being driven away from the inheritance of Yahweh and caused to forsake Yahweh, "O Yahweh, why dost Thou make us to err from Thy ways, and hardenest our heart from fearing Thee? Return for the sake of Thy servants, for the sake of the tribes of Thine inheritance (שִׁבְטֵי נַחֲלָתֶךָ)," lxiii. 17. Cheyne's comment *ad loc.* is, "It is as if the Jews would throw the responsibility of their errors upon Jehovah; and this in spite of the encouraging invitations contained in this very book. They speak as if it is not they who need to return to Jehovah (lv. 7), but Jehovah who is reluctant to return to them; as if, instead of 'feeding his flock like a shepherd' (xl. 11), he has driven it out of the safe fold into the 'howling wilderness.'" How accurately Cheyne's description fits the case of the poor cast-out Samaritans! In the following verse, if correctly restored, they plead as a further reason the desolation of the temple, which they felt could not be restored by the unaided Jews of Jerusalem, "Why do the wicked march over Thy Holy Place, and our adversaries trample Thy Sanctuary?" The 'wicked' and the 'adversaries' were the heathen living in and about Jerusalem, who were a considerable power in the community, including as they very likely did a certain number of Persian officials. Verse 19 gives the climax: the Samaritans were called heathen. The words, "From everlasting Thou hast not ruled over them; Thy name was not named upon them," are a long synonym for "the heathen." Compare Deut. xxviii. 10, "And all the peoples of the earth

6—2

shall see that the name of Yahweh is named upon
Thee, and they shall be afraid of Thee." So the prophet
says, הָיִינוּ "מֵעוֹלָם לֹא־מָשַׁלְתָּ בָּם לֹא־נִקְרָא שִׁמְךָ
"עֲלֵיהֶם "We have become 'From everlasting Thou
hast not ruled over them; Thy name was not named
upon them,'" *i.e.* "We have become heathen." R.V.
adds the word 'as' in order to make sense. Cheyne
says, "The meaning of this half-verse is very uncertain.
The omission of 'like' constitutes a serious difficulty
in the ordinary rendering[1]." But taken as above there
is no need to add anything: the Samaritans were not
told they were 'heathenish' but 'heathen.' For the
grammatical construction compare Gen. xxxi. 40,
הָיִיתִי בַיּוֹם אֲכָלַנִי חֹרֶב וְקֶרַח בַּלָּיְלָה " I was ' In the
day the drought consumed me, and the frost by
night,'" *i.e.* "I was in the condition of being consumed
by drought by day and by frost by night[2]."

Chapter lxiv. does not give any such clear tokens
of the Samaritan origin of the section, but it is quite
in accordance with such an origin, and gives several
illustrations of it. Verse 5 (E.V. 6) "And we have all

---

[1] Knobel avoided adding the word 'like' in his translation, if not
altogether in his comment. His note is, "aus dem heiligen Lande
vertrieben und in ein fremdes Land gebracht *sind wir die, welche du
von Ewigkeit nicht beherrscht hast, auf welche dein Name nicht genannt
worden ist*, d. h. wir sind in einer Lage, als wärest du niemals unser
Herr gewesen und als hiessen und wären wir nicht Jehova's Volk; wir
sind und heissen ganz Unterthanen der Babylonier."

[2] Gesenius-Kautsch, § 143*a*, note 1, says, "Gen. xxxi. 40 erscheint
statt des Subjekts ein Verbalsatz (הָיִיתִי ich war), der dann durch
einen anderen Verbalsatz expliziert wird."

become as one that is unclean, and all our righteous acts are as a polluted garment," is in reference to the charge laid against them by Haggai (ii. 14) that they were unclean. It almost seems as if the prophet were taking Haggai at his word and saying, "Yes, we confess our uncleanness, but it is Yahweh's wont to forgive His people when they repent." This sense of guilt is certainly shown in the next verse, "there is none that calleth upon Thy name, that stirreth up himself to take hold of Thee." The remaining words of the verse, "For Thou hast hid Thy face from us, and Thou hast delivered us up (reading וַתְּמַגְּנֵנוּ) into the power of our iniquities," are intended as an explanation of lxiii. 17—the prophet had said too much in suggesting that Yahweh was causing the people to err; if they were prevented from worshipping Yahweh it must be by reason of their former sins. The repeated use of the first person plural, and the word 'all, suggests that the prophet is guarding against the exclusion of any—"*we all* are the work of Thy hand" (*v.* 7), "*we all* are Thy people" (*v.* 8), "*our* holy and *our* beautiful house where *our* fathers praised Thee" (*v.* 10), "all *our* sacred spots" (so probably translate מַחֲמַדֵּינוּ) (*v.* 10), and perhaps even the "we all" of *v.* 5 is a gentle hint that Jews as well as Samaritans are besmirched with sin. The remarkable phrase עָרֵי קָדְשֶׁךָ "Thy holy cities" in lxiv. 9 (E. V. 10) finds an easy explanation if the speaker was from North Israel: he might quite probably agree that Jerusalem was Yahweh's chief sanctuary, but he would most likely also class Bethel and Samaria among the holy cities. This seems an

easier explanation than that of Gesenius that since the
land was called 'holy' (as in Zech. ii. 16, E.V. 12) the
sum-total of cities might also be called 'holy.' "Wilt
Thou restrain Thyself (תִּתְאַפַּק) for these things?" in
lxiv. 11, and "Restrain not the yearning of Thy bowels
and Thy tender mercies" (taking Oort's emendation
אַל תִּתְאַפָּק) in lxiii. 15, are in striking contrast with
xlii. 14, "I have long time holden my peace, I have
been still and refrained myself (אֶתְאַפָּק): as a woman
with child will I cry out, etc.," and the situation here
suggested for lxiii. 7–lxiv. amply explains the difference. Deutero-Isaiah in that earlier passage had
declared that Yahweh was bestirring Himself on
behalf of His people. To our Samaritan prophet it
seemed that men like Haggai and Zechariah lacked
faith in Yahweh, for instead of expecting His intervention directly they were only looking for Him
to intervene by some intermediary—the 'Chosen of
Yahweh,' the 'Servant of Yahweh,' or whatever they
might call him—and it was for this reason that our
prophet called to mind the fact that of old it was
Yahweh Himself who saved His people and not a
messenger or angel (Is. lxiii. 9).

II. *An Embassage from Bethel.*

The Samaritan prophet was not the only Samaritan
to be stirred into action by the attitude of the Jews.
An incident has been recorded as an introduction to
one of Zechariah's prophecies, and though the text is
in a poor state of preservation it is sufficient to tell the
main event. The passage is Zech. vii. 1–7. The first

verse has the clause, "The word of Yahweh came unto Zechariah," inserted, and also the name 'Kislew' of the month. These insertions betray themselves by interfering with the sense and by the fact that in verse 4 Zechariah is speaking in the first person. Verse 2 provides greater difficulties. It begins וַיִּשְׁלַח

בֵּית־אֵל "And Bethel sent." Commentators generally object to taking this unamended as it stands. Mitchell says, "if Bethel be made the subject there is the objection that places were not personified by the Hebrews, except in poetry." This is not quite accurate, for in I Sam. vi. 13 we read, וּבֵית שֶׁמֶשׁ קֹצְרִים קְצִיר חִטִּים

בָּעֵמֶק "Bethshemesh were reaping their wheat harvest in the valley," which only differs by its plural predicate from a poetic expression like Job i. 15, וַתִּפֹּל שְׁבָא

וַתִּקָּחֵם "And Seba fell (upon them) and carried them away." Mitchell would amend to אַנְשֵׁי בֵיתְאֵל "men of Bethel," and van Hoonacker to בֵּית יִשְׂרָאֵל "House of Israel." R.V., presumably without emending the text, translates it as "*they of* Bethel." The names that follow in the same verse, "Sarezer and Regem Melek and his men" are probably not original. Mitchell thinks that the words are a later insertion, and suggests that when first inserted it read רַב מַג, Rab-mag, which still appears in the Syriac version. The easiest supposition is that originally the names of the embassage were not mentioned, but that someone, wishing to make it quite clear that the embassage was heathen, added a heathen name from Jer. xxxix. 3, שַׂרְאֶצֶר [נֵרְגַל]

רַב־מָג...(ה)מֶלֶךְ "[Nergal]-sarezer Rab-Mag of the king." With the emendations thus suggested in the first two verses, we get the following text, "It came to pass in the fourth year of Darius, on the fourth day of the ninth month, that Bethel sent to entreat the favour of Yahweh, (and) to speak unto the priests of the house of Yahweh Sabaoth, and unto the prophets, saying, 'Am I to weep in the fifth month, separating myself, as I have done these so many years?'" Zechariah gave an answer at once, and returned again to the question in vii. 18–23. In that latter passage he speaks of peoples and nations and inhabitants of cities coming in the future to intreat the favour of Yahweh, and this confirms our belief that vii. 1, 2 tells of an embassage from Bethel. Now Bethel was the once famous sanctuary in the Northern Kingdom, where Yahweh had been worshipped under the symbol of a golden calf, and the embassage was therefore from people whose loyalty to Yahweh would be suspect in the eyes of the Jews of Jerusalem. Bethel is actually mentioned in II Kings xvii. 28 as one of the places where the Samaritans practised their mixed worship.

A good deal of support has been given by commentators to the suggestion that we have in Zech. vii. 2 a man's name Bethelsharusur, of which the first part is the name of a deity known from various sources, and especially recently as a deity who was worshipped by the Elephantine Jews alongside of Yahu[1]. But even if accepted, this translation does not make the passage

---

[1] Deities Ashim-bethel and Anath-bethel are mentioned in Sachau's papyrus 18, and proper names of men compounded with Bethel in papyri 17, 25, 34.

clear, and the suggestion put forward above seems more probable. One of the places where 'Bethel' possibly appears as the name of a deity is Jer. xlviii. 13, "And Moab shall be ashamed of Chemosh as the house of Israel was ashamed of Bethel their confidence," and S. A. Cook remarks on this that "Bethel stands to Israel in precisely the same relation as Chemosh to Moab[1]." In the light of this, the embassage, if headed by a man named Bethelsharusur, would still presumably be from the Northern country. Although van Hoonacker emends away 'Bethel' into 'House of Israel,' yet he understands it similarly as an embassage on the part of the Northern, *i.e.* Samaritan, population which affected to have remained faithful to the worship of Yahweh. He says[2] "Il semble ultérieurement que 'la maison d'Israel' de notre *v.* 2 aura représenté, non pas le peuple juif en général, mais en particulier cet élément de la population du Nord, c'est-à-dire de Samarie, qui affectait d'être demeurée fidèle au culte de Jahvé (Ezr. iv. 2). Ainsi comprend-on mieux que le but assigné à la délégation soit tout d'abord 'de rendre Jahvé favorable' לְחַלּוֹת אֶת־פְּנֵי יְהוָה; une formule qui ne prouverait rien par elle-même, mais qui est employée plus loin dans le discours de Zacharie viii. 21, 23 pour *les peuples étrangers* qui se rallieront au culte de Jahvé." Some seventy years later, in the time of Nehemiah, we are told there were 123 or 223 Jews in Bethel and Ai (Neh. vii. 32 = Ezr. ii. 28), but this proves

---

[1] "Significance of the Elephantine Papyri," *American Journal of Theology*, July 1915, p. 370.
[2] *Les Douze Petits Prophètes*, p. 637.

nothing about the state of affairs in 518 B.C., for these
Jews may have been later arrivals. At any rate the
mass of the population of Bethel was not of the tribe
of Judah. Now remembering the charges that had been
laid against the Samaritans, that they were not Israelites (Is. lxiii. 16), and that they had nothing to do with
the Israelites in building the temple (Ezr. iv. 3), we
recognize that the question of the embassage from
Bethel was closely connected with the controversy as
to whether they were Israelites or not. They asked
whether they were to continue observing the fast of
the fifth month which commemorated the exile of
Judah (II Kings xxv. 8, Jer. lii. 12). The fact that
they had observed it all along might be taken to prove
that they were Jews, but on the other hand if they were
not Jews why should they keep the fast? Zechariah's
first answer (vii. 5) was directed not merely to the men
of Bethel but to all the population ('the people of the
land and the priests'). Besides the fast of the fifth
month, Zechariah also mentioned the fast of the seventh
month, which is said to have commemorated the murder
of Gedaliah by Ishmael (Jer. xli. 1–10). As Ishmael
killed forty Samaritans at the same time it is quite
likely that the Samaritans especially kept the fast.
The embassage from Bethel had only mentioned the
fast commemorating the exile of Judah; but Zechariah
reminds them also of their especially Samaritan fast,
and says that their fasts were not to Yahweh and their
feasts were to themselves. That is, they could not
argue as to their loyalty to Yahweh from having kept
the fasts and feasts. Zechariah returned to the subject
again in viii. 18. In viii. 19 he said that for the house of

Judah the fasts would become feasts, and the stress laid on the house of Judah seems to be specially intended to exclude the Samaritans. Then in verses 20–23 he dealt with foreigners, saying that they would come to seek Yahweh. Probably he imagined this as happening only after the Messiah had come, just as 'in that day' (ii. 11) must mean the day of Messiah's appearing. At any rate, as far as Samaritans were concerned, it was made quite clear that their hope of acceptance was not to rest in a claim to be Israelites, but they must come as suppliant heathen.

III. *The Last Words of Deutero-Isaiah.*

Chapters lxv. and lxvi. of Isaiah form a single prophecy, which throws a great deal of light on the religious conditions of the time in which it was written. From lxvi. 1 it is evident at first sight that the prophecy dates from a time when a project was afoot to build a temple to Yahweh. One would naturally think of the temple built by Zerubbabel, but commentators have tried to avoid this, perhaps feeling that since God wished to have the temple rebuilt at Jerusalem the plan could not have been opposed by one of God's prophets. Thus Hitzig and others thought the prophet was opposing a plan to build a temple to Yahweh in Babylon, while in more recent times Cheyne and Duhm have connected the prophecy with the building of a rival temple by the Samaritans on Mount Gerizim. They have felt that the prophet was striving, not against the temple and cultus of Yahweh generally, but only against the particular proposal; but they have had to confess that the prophet's arguments would equally well apply against any temple for Yahweh. Thus Knobel says[1], "The author brings forward a reason which properly speaking would avail also against the building of a temple in Jerusalem in so far as that was thought of as a dwelling of Yahweh." Cheyne, with greater detail, says[2], "The same writer (probably) who has just spoken so harshly of the Samaritans because they have refused to adopt the Jewish law [Is. lxv. 1, 2 according to Cheyne's interpretation], now censures them for wishing to build a central sanctuary of their own, and bases this censure on a principle which, regarded logically, is just as adverse to the claims of the temple at Jerusalem....The explanation is that post-exilic Jewish religion is to a large extent a fusion of inconsistent elements, of prophetic and priestly origin, respectively....And so this writer, though he holds that not even the temple at Jerusalem is worthy of the Divine Creator, yet expostulates with those who plan the erection of another temple elsewhere. It is only in the temple so lately rebuilt that the right worshippers are to be found, viz., the humble and obedient Jewish believers. Let the Samaritans renounce their self-chosen and often abominable customs, and submit to the Law, and then it will be permitted to them to worship God in a temple made with hands." One wonders whether even ignorant Samaritans would be so lacking in logic as to fail to see through such an argument against their building a temple. Would not the prophet rather have appealed to the fact that Yahweh had commanded one sanctuary

---

[1] *Der Prophet Jesaia, ad loc.*, 3rd ed. 1861.
[2] *Jewish Religious Life after the Exile*, pp. 28, 29.

and one only in the land? That is what Duhm thinks
the prophet meant, but certainly there is no suggestion
of the idea in the chapter before us. Commenting on
lxvi. 1 Duhm says, "In the olden days the Deity has
one sanctuary, only in the place where He dwells and
has made known His dwelling by a vision. Since the
time of Deuteronomy the faithful Jew believed that
Yahweh had indicated the Hill of Zion alone as His
dwelling." However prevalent that idea may have
been we cannot read it into this chapter where it is
not mentioned. A few voices have been raised against
this current misinterpretation. Wellhausen says[1], "In
Isaiah lxvi. 1–4 a protest is uttered against the renewal
of the temple and the sacrificial cultus. A sense is
usually squeezed out of these verses which directly
contradicts the wording, in that the adjective 'illegitimate' is falsely inserted." And Montgomery[2], after
referring to Duhm's view, says "Despite the assent
which has been gained for this view, I must hold to
the interpretation that is as old as St Stephen (Acts vii.
48 ff.), and which is still maintained by Wellhausen,
that the passage lxvi. 1 ff. is a prophetic flight concerning spiritual worship which has its parallels in the
Prophets and the Psalms, the full fruitage coming in
Christianity." This was substantially the belief of
Bishop Lowth[3] who said, "God admonishes them that
the Most High dwelleth not in temples made with
hands; and that a mere external worship, how dili-
gently soever attended, when accompanied with wicked

---

[1] *Israelitische und jüdische Geschichte*, 5te Aufl. 1904, p. 167 note.
[2] *The Samaritans*, pp. 70, 71.
[3] *On Isaiah, ad loc.*, 11th ed. 1835.

and idolatrous practices in the worshippers, would never be accepted by him," though Lowth curiously thought that the passage referred to the building of Herod's temple. Montgomery's opposition to the current interpretation is largely because it would make the Samaritan community a heathen body, whereas when the Samaritans first emerge clearly into the light of history they appear as a sect of Judaism. On page 71, note, he says, "If Duhm's view is correct, an explanation is required for the transition of the idolatrous Samaritan community into a sect imitative of Judaism, a phenomenon, which, as already remarked, would be a spiritual marvel."

The conclusion that Is. lxv., lxvi. has reference to the building of the temple at Jerusalem, *i.e.* the building in the reign of Darius I, brings this section into the circle of literature which we have already considered. As confirmatory evidence we find that this section is in some respects an answer to the Samaritan Plaint of lxiii. 7–lxiv. One verse, lxvi. 5, definitely refers to the rejection of the Samaritans, "Hear the word of Yahweh, ye that tremble at His word: Your brethren that hate you, that cast you out for my name's sake, have said, 'Let Yahweh be glorified, that we may see your joy,' but they shall be ashamed." If we ask, Who were the people who were cast out? the answer can only be the Samaritans. Their proffered help had been rejected and they were treated as if they had no share in the inheritance of Yahweh. But on what grounds had they been cast out? We have seen that the reason stated for the refusal of their help was that it was excluded by the terms of Cyrus' decree, and we have

suggested that the real motive was smouldering tribal
jealousy. But we may be sure that the Jews in rejecting
the Samaritans believed that they were performing the
will of Yahweh. That is exactly what the prophet says
here: they that cast you out for my name's sake said
"Let Yahweh be glorified," and then sarcastically "that
we may see your joy." But the Jews were wrong in supposing that their action would glorify Yahweh, for, adds
the prophet, "they shall be ashamed." The prophet
also utters another note of rebuke in using the word
'brethren'—the Jews were brothers of the Samaritans
whom they cast out. It may be noted that the verb
נִדָּה, which only occurs once elsewhere in the O.T.,
is used in New Hebrew for 'excommunicate.' Montgomery, referring to this verse, says (p. 71) "It is to
be noted that the prophet belongs to those that are
excommunicated, not to the triumphant party which
cast out the Shechemites." This however is arguing a
little too much from the verse. The prophet certainly
did not belong to the triumphant party which cast out
the Samaritans, for he evidently did not hold with them
at all, but the fact that he showed sympathy towards
the Samaritans does not prove that he was one of
them, and this question must be further considered,
and we must remember that prophets often hold independent positions and do not belong to any party. At
first sight lxvi. 5 might be thought to be like li. 7,
addressed to Jews and comforting them for the wanton
reproaches of the heathen. But in the earlier passage
the persecutors are simply described as 'men,' אֱנוֹשׁ,
i.e. presumably the heathen peoples mentioned in li. 4,

5, whereas here the persecutors are 'brethren,' and they
behave thus 'for my name's sake' and with intent that
'Yahweh may be glorified.'

The whole of the section lxv.,lxvi. is not addressed to
the Samaritan Yahweh-worshippers, but now that we
have seen where the prophet's sympathies lay we can
go carefully through the chapters.   Chapter lxv. begins
by Yahweh saying that He is holding out His hands
to attract rebellious people who are not seeking Him.
It is difficult to see what meaning can be intended by
the R.V. translation of lxv. 1, "I am inquired of by
them that asked not *for me*," which is merely a self-
contradiction. The verbs must be given the sense which
sometimes attaches to the niph'al of allowing something
to affect oneself, the so-called niph'al tolerativum[1]. It
then reads, " I am (ready) to be enquired of by those
who asked not (for me) ; I am (ready) to be found by
those that sought me not. I said ' Here am I,' ' Here
am I' unto a nation that hath not called on my name."
(With the versions, including R.V. mg., and most commentators, we read קָרָא or קֹרֵא 'calleth' instead of
the M.T. קֹרָא ' is called.') If there were any doubt as
to the translation of verse 1, the translation given above
would be shown to be correct by verse 2, which makes
the sense clear that there is a certain class of people
who do not worship Yahweh and that He is willing to
accept worship from them. The succeeding verses show
plainly the religious practices of these people to have
been purely heathen. They sacrificed things forbidden
in the Jewish cultus, sacrificed apart from any lawful

---

[1] Gesenius-Kautsch, § 51 *c*.

sanctuary, believed that in their mystic rites they at-
tained a peculiar holiness, and offered worship to Gad
and Meni. Now although these acts are purely heathen
they are predicated of people of whom better things
might have been expected. The term 'provoketh me
to my face' in lxv. 3 indicates Israelites who have rejected Yahweh: the verb הַכְעִים occurs about forty
times of Israelites provoking Yahweh to anger by
deserting Him and serving foreign gods, and once
(Neh. iii. 37, E.V. iv. 5) of Samaritans provoking
Yahweh by trying to hinder the building of the walls
of Jerusalem. It is never used of heathen. Then again
the expression "ye that forsake Yahweh and forget
my holy mountain" indicates that these people are
renegades who had once been worshippers of Yahweh
and had once recognized the sanctity of Zion. It may
therefore be regarded as certain that the class of people
here addressed were, in some measure at least, Israelites;
and it is only natural to suppose that they were half-
castes, part Israelite and part Gentile. We have conjectured above that most of the Jewish population had
some admixture of Gentile blood, but these people referred to here would be such as were more Gentile than
Jew, more attached to heathenism than Judaism. Such
people might easily ignore the Israelite national Deity.
At the same time the prophet has hopes for them, and
that is why Yahweh is pictured as having His arms
stretched out towards them. Of some the prophet is
quite confident; they are 'servants' of Yahweh and
will prove a faithful remnant (lxv. 8, 9). And inasmuch
as they are spoken of as "from Jacob and from Judah"

they must include half-castes not only of Judaea but also of Samaria (Jacob, *i.e.* Israel, the Northern Kingdom[1]). Duhm commenting on verse 8 quite rightly points out that this could not have been written after the activity of Nehemiah, who so sharply distinguished between the pure and the mixed stock. But he certainly is not correct in thinking that the words of rebuke were directed against the Jews of the land as distinct from the returned exiles, and that the native Israelites would be accepted into the community if they would accept the law as it was understood by the returned exiles[2]. It is clear that the prophet is not upholding a new law against old-fashioned Yahweh-worshippers who are unacquainted with the new law, but that he is upholding Yahweh worship, as taught and practised at least since the days of the first literary prophets, against worshippers of false gods. The point that these false worshippers were still regarded, or still regarded themselves, as Israelites, is brought out forcibly in lxv. 15—so debased had the name Israel become owing to their evil ways that it was even

[1] 'Jacob' is sometimes used for Judah as opposed to the Northern Kingdom, *e.g.* Ps. lxxvii. 16 (E. V. 15) "the sons of Jacob and Joseph," Micah iii. 8 " to declare unto Jacob his transgression and to Israel his sin." But sometimes 'Jacob' stands for the Northern Kingdom as opposed to Judah, *e.g.* Amos vii. 2, 5 "How shall Jacob stand?" (Amos only preached in the Northern Kingdom), Micah i. 5 "What is the transgression of Jacob? is it not Samaria? And what are the high places of Judah? are they not Jerusalem?" So also Is. ix. 7 (E. V. 8) and probably Hosea x. 11, xii. 3 (E. V. 2).

[2] Duhm on Is. lxv. 1, "Auch für die feindlichen Brüder, jene Judäer und Samarier, die ausser der Gola in Palästina lebten, war Jahve da, sie hatten also in die Gemeinde aufgenommen werden können (so gut wie die bene-nekar lvi. 1 ff.), wenn sie dem Gesetz, wie es die Gola verstand, sich unterworfen hätten."

possible that 'Israel' might be used as a curse, like
'Sodom and Gomorrah,' and in that case Yahweh would
find a new name for the faithful ones among His chosen
people. The singular 'your name' precludes Duhm's
suggestion that it was the names of such men as Sanballat and Tobiah which would become a reviling. In
Is. lxii. 2, probably written about 450 B.C., some seventy
years later than this prophecy, the same idea appears
of Yahweh giving Israel a new and better name. A
fuller meaning is seen in lxv. 15 when the chapters
lxv. and lxvi. are regarded as in some sense a reply to
the Samaritan Plaint of lxiii. 7–lxiv. The Samaritans
had complained (lxiii. 16, 19) that they were denied
the name of Israel. The prophet who wrote lxv., lxvi.
replied that the name was not everything; even the
sacred name of Israel might be debased, but God could
supply a better one if need be. And then to press
home this lesson he quoted from Gen. xxii. 18 but
with a significant alteration. Instead of saying "All
the nations of the earth shall bless themselves *in thy
seed*" he said "He that blesseth himself in the earth
(*i.e.* of course 'those all over the world who bless themselves') shall bless himself *in the God of truth*." Antici-
pating St John the Baptist and St Paul[1] by nearly six
centuries the prophet saw that physical descent from
Abraham was not the real source of blessing. In so
far as the Samaritans were true worshippers of Yahweh
they need not fret if Abraham and Israel did not recognize them. There is considerable skill in the way
the prophet first denounced false worshippers with
tremendous vigour, lest in speaking favourably of

[1] Mt. iii. 9, Gal. iii. 7, Rom. ii. 28, 29, etc.

Samaritans he should be thought to be compromising with the heathenism practised by many of them, and then, having safe-guarded the uniqueness of Yahweh, he turned with the utmost charity to the faithful worshippers whose only fault was that they dwelt in Samaria or had some admixture of foreign blood. From here the prophet goes on (lxv. 17–25) with an apocalyptic picture of the new Jerusalem. But what a contrast from the apocalyptic of Haggai! This prophet would found his glorious future on the present: the peace of wolf and lamb will be the outcome of the peace of Jew and Samaritan. Is it fancy to see in this prophet's attitude towards the half-castes—an attitude of patience even with the most desperate renegades—the missionary policy of Deutero-Isaiah? And is it a fancy to imagine that Deutero-Isaiah had come back from Babylonia to see the beginning of the restoration of Israel, and to try to put into practice his great conception of a restored Israel becoming the missionary of the world?

In chapter lxvi. he turned to those who were contemplating building the temple again. It is not likely that he was altogether against the scheme, but he did distinctly see a danger in it. There was a real danger of thinking of the Creator of all things as dwelling within four walls, as Haggai seems to have done when he compared the house of God with the houses of the people, "Is it a time for you yourselves to dwell in your panelled houses while this house lieth waste?" (Hag. i. 4). So he brings forward his great plea for a spiritual religion (lxvi. 1, 2):

"Thus saith Yahweh: The heaven is my throne and the earth the footstool of my feet.

> Where is the house that ye will build me, and
> where the sanctuary that shall be my resting
> place?
>
> And all these things (*i.e.* all created things) my
> hand made them, and so all these things came
> into being, saith Yahweh.
>
> But to this one will I look, even to the poor and
> contrite of spirit, and that trembleth at my
> word."

Some comments are needed on the above translation.
מָקוֹם is translated 'sanctuary' as in II Kings v. 11 and
Ezr. viii. 17 (see p. 53). כָּל־אֵלֶּה "all these things"
must be taken, with Cheyne, as referring to the heaven
and earth just mentioned. It cannot be translated 'all
this' ('dies alles,' Duhm) referring to the temple.
Duhm says that כָּל־אֵלֶּה stands clearly in parallel with
אֶל־זֶה 'to this one' (*v.* 2b), but there can be no verbal
parallel either between all created things and humble
men or between the temple and humble men. The
contrast is rather expressed than stated: it is that
Yahweh is so great that He cannot live in a house,
but yet He can pay attention to the humble of heart.
Then follows a verse, which for its terseness has been
often misunderstood, but which is clear the moment
it is realized that the prophet is teaching a spiritual
religion and is dreading a temple cultus that will be
merely external:

"Killing an ox   : slaying a man
 Sacrificing a sheep   : breaking a dog's neck
 Offering an oblation : [pouring out] swine's blood
 Burning frankincense : blessing an idol.

Just as they have chosen their ways,
And their soul delighteth in their abominations,
So will I choose their delusions,
And will bring their fears upon them."

Earlier on (lxv. 3–7) the prophet had spoken his mind about those who practised heathen rites. He did not look on them simply as meaningless acts, but as overt rebellion against Yahweh. Now we are startled to read—and he meant his readers to be startled—that the rites of lawful cultus are comparable with heathen rites. The prophet was acquainted with the writings of Isaiah (lxv. 25, reminiscent of Is. xi. 6–9, shows that), and he would remember the brave words of Is. i. 14, "Your new moons and your appointed feasts my soul hateth; they are a trouble unto me; I am weary to bear them." Probably neither prophet really intended to go so far as to forbid the cultus; probably both of them were distressed at the cultus regarded as an end in itself. From here our prophet goes on with words of comfort for the Samaritans who have been cast out (lxvi. 5). He is only speaking to the *faithful* Samaritans, those who "tremble at His word"—the expression that has just been used in verse 2 of those to whom Yahweh will look. They will find comfort in the fact that the wicked will be brought to shame even though they wear the garb of orthodoxy. The prophet had pleaded for a wider outlook, something more than the mere rebuilding of the temple and the re-establishment of the cultus. And now giving vent to his poetic fancy he hears the city (whose walls still lay in ruins) crying out, and the temple (also in ruins) crying out, but crying not merely for their own restoration, but for righteousness and prosperity. The mention of the temple does not prove that it was standing, any more than the mention of the city. As a matter of fact one would expect a cry of anguish demanding recompence of enemies rather from desolate ruins than from well-appointed buildings. The restoration of Israel is taking place already (*vv.* 7–9). Those who love Jerusalem and have mourned with her in her affliction are now to rejoice in her restoration; they shall receive the blessings of Jerusalem and be comforted in her; and their glory like an overflowing stream shall flow into Jerusalem. Has any commentator asked who, or what nation, mourned over Jerusalem in her affliction? Certainly not Edom, nor Ammon, nor Moab, nor Philistia[1], nor Babylonia. Of one people only is it recorded that they wept for the captivity of Judah—and that was the Samaritans! It was Bethel that said, "Am I to weep in the fifth month, separating myself, as I have done these so many years?" (Zech. vii. 3). Zechariah's scornful answer we have seen. But this is Deutero-Isaiah's answer, that they who mourned over Jerusalem in her affliction shall rejoice with her in her joy. The next few verses deal with the wrath of Yahweh which will be visited on the idolaters, and then in *vv.* 18–22 the prophet brings out his full missionary programme—"to gather together all the nations and the tongues; and they shall come and they shall see my glory. And I will set on them a sign (reminiscent of the sign that He set on Cain, Gen. iv. 15), and those of them who escape (*i.e.* from Yahweh's judgment, almost equivalent as Duhm says to 'die Auserwählte,' 'the Elect') I will

_____
[1] See Ezek. xxv.

send unto the nations, to Tarshish, Pul, and Lud
Meshech, and to Tubal (so Greek; cf. Ezek. xxvii, 13
xxxviii. 2, xxxix. 1), and Javan, to the distant coasts
that have not heard my fame nor seen my glory; and
they shall declare my glory among the nations. And
they shall bring all your brethren out of all the nations
for an offering to Yahweh, upon horses, and in chariots
and in litters, and upon mules, and upon swift beasts
unto my holy mountain Jerusalem, saith Yahweh, as
the children of Israel bring the offering in a clean
vessel unto the house of Yahweh." Possibly we should
infer from the word פְּלִיטִים (*v.* 19) that all this is only
to take place after Yahweh's judgment, but we have
seen that the prophet is willing to welcome the Samaritans already. For him the only condition is that they
shall "tremble at the word of Yahweh." If they do
that they will be 'brethren' (lxvi. 20), as the faithful
Samaritans are already (lxvi. 5). Of the nations when
they are brought in, some will be taken for priests or
Levites. That is undoubtedly the meaning of verse 21;
it cannot refer to returned Israelites, for if they were
already of priestly or Levitical descent they would not
need to be chosen as such.

The possibility that Deutero-Isaiah was the author
of lxvi. was shown unconsciously by Duhm in his comment on Is. liv. 4, for he shows that if Deutero-Isaiah had
been consistent he would have denounced the idea of
Yahweh having an earthly dwelling place. He says,
"Since the Exile Yahweh dwelt no longer in Zion,
whither indeed, according to lii. 8, He did not return
until the liberation. Equally truly He did not dwell,

according to Deutero-Isaiah, among the exiles, nor indeed among the Diaspora scattered all over the world, but He dwelt in heaven (xl. 22) and had at the moment no dwelling place on earth.   That Deutero-Isaiah did not denounce the latter, in spite of all his Universalism and all his enthusiasm for Yahweh's greatness, shows how tenaciously the historical condition of affairs was held on to, and how the national interests of Israel asserted Israel's precedence in religion even side by side with the most ideal and most unprejudiced manner of thought."

It is a great temptation to seek illustrations from the Psalms for any historical period, but the attempt is fraught with danger because the indications of date and origin are so scanty in the Psalms.   As long as the dates of the Psalms are so uncertain, and until there is some agreement as to the course of post-exilic history, it would probably be wisest not to attempt to fit the Psalms into the provisional framework of the history. Just one suggestion however is thrown out here for further consideration.   There are reasons for connecting Ps. lxxx. not only with the early post-exilic period, but also with the Samaritans.   Briggs dates it 'early Persian period,' and says that it is "a prayer of Israel for a divine advent of salvation...that the Shepherd of Israel would shine forth before Northern Israel," and again, "North Israel seems to be prominent in the mind of the poet as often in the Asaph Psalter lxxvii. 16, lxxviii. 67, lxxxi. 6; emphasized in 'before Ephraim and Manasseh,' the two sons of Joseph, and standing for the chief tribes of the North[1]."   Our text as it stands

[1] C. A. Briggs, *The Psalms*, Vol. II. pp. 201, 203.

at present says " Before Ephraim, and Benjamin, and Manasseh," which is one word too many according to the metre; and of the four words the one most easily regarded as an addition is וּבְנְיָמִן 'and Benjamin.' The name Benjamin was evidently added by someone who connected Benjamin with the Northern Kingdom; it was really on the border line between the two kingdoms, but its principal towns, Bethel, Gilgal and Jericho, as Kirkpatrick reminds us[1], belonged to the Northern Kingdom. It is striking in Ps. lxxx. 2 to find mention of 'Israel' and 'Joseph' without the corresponding 'Jacob' or 'Judah' that we find in the other Asaph Psalms (lxxvii. 16, lxxviii. 71, lxxxi. 5, lxxvi. 2)—" O Shepherd of Israel, give ear! Thou that leadest Joseph as a flock." The refrain of the Psalm, verses 4, 8, 15, 20, "Yahweh Sabaoth, turn us again! and cause Thy face to shine that we may be saved," is perhaps reminiscent of Ephraim's prayer in Jer. xxxi. 18, "Turn Thou me that I may be turned," which is quoted also in Lam. v. 21, "Turn Thou us, O Yahweh, unto Thee, that we may be turned." Kirkpatrick says, "The special interest shown in the tribes of the Northern Kingdom (v. 2) may have been due to the connexion of the author with one of those tribes; but it is sufficiently accounted for by the prominence given to Israel's restoration in Jeremiah and Ezekiel." In Is. lxiii. 15 occur the words הַבֵּט מִשָּׁמַיִם וּרְאֵה " Look down from heaven and behold," on which Cheyne comments as follows: " The peculiar Hebrew original occurs again in Ps. lxxx. 15, and nowhere else. Dr Weir [of Glasgow, to whose

[1] *ad loc.*

lecture notes Cheyne had access] adds that the whole
of the Psalm may be compared with this section of the
prophecy." We have already seen reason to attribute
that section of Isaiah to a Samaritan prophet writing
at the time of the rebuilding of the temple. Ps. lxxx.
shows interest in Northern Israel, and in Northern
Israel alone, and it would appear to date from the same
period. The similarity of language and thought noted
by Weir and Cheyne between the Psalm and the
Isaianic passage confirms the suspicion that Ps. lxxx.
was produced by a Samaritan psalmist under the same
conditions as produced Is. lxiii. 7–lxiv. It is equally
clear that the whole of the Asaph Psalter was *not*
written by Samaritans, witness only Ps. lxxviii. 67, 68
" And He refused the tent of Joseph, and chose not
the tribe of Ephraim. But He chose the tribe of Judah,
the Mount Zion which He loved." Still, the Asaph
Psalms do show an interest in the Northern Kingdom
that does not appear elsewhere, and this may be accounted for by supposing that the Guild of Asaph dwelt
at Bethel or somewhere else in the Northern district.

The offer of the Samaritans to assist in the building
of the temple was a test of Israel's sense of missionary
vocation. We have no reason to suppose that the offer
was made from any but the highest motives. The
Chronicler undoubtedly bore no love towards the
Samaritans, and it is evidently his anti-Samaritan
hand which framed the words of Ezr. iv. 2. But even
so, perverted as the sentence has been by the Chronicler's
bias, there is not a word to which exception could be
taken; the whole sentence is courteous and devout:
" Let us build with you, for we seek your God, as ye

do; and we have been sacrificing unto Him since the days of Asarhaddon king of Assyria who brought us up hither." It might of course have been said that they had broken the Deuteronomic law by sacrificing elsewhere than in Jerusalem; but reason would have said that that law was not binding when the temple in Jerusalem lay in ruins. At any rate, the offer to help rebuild the temple suggested a readiness to obey the Deuteronomic law as soon as they were able.

Here was the opportunity that Deutero-Isaiah had looked forward to, of people coming and claiming to belong to Yahweh and attesting themselves as Israelites (Is. xliv. 5), people coming to the Jews and saying "Surely God is in thee" (Is. xlv. 14). Here was the promised opportunity of teaching the weary (Is. l. 4). With the coldest hardest words the opportunity was rejected—unless perchance the Chronicler has made his heroes more brutal than they really were—"Ye have nothing to do with us to build a house unto our God; but we ourselves together will build unto Yahweh the God of Israel, as Cyrus the king of Persia hath commanded us" (Ezr. iv. 3). The limit of faithlessness was reached when the Jews supported their refusal by a pretended obedience to the foreign civil ruler. Irresistibly one is reminded of that cry of their descendants, "We have no king but Caesar" (Jn. xix. 15). The circumstances were similar—the condemnation of the guiltless in face of the truth, and the decision of a religious question by a suggestion of *lèse-majesté* towards a heathen ruler. It is remarkable how the refusal of the Samaritan help was a policy deliberately adopted by the whole nation. According to Ezr. iv. 3 the decision was communicated to the Samaritans by Zerubbabel the civil governor, Jeshua the high priest, and the heads of fathers' houses—the most representative body of men that could be imagined, representing State, Church, and people. If we follow Rothstein in his theory about the book of Haggai, even the prophetic party was not unrepresented, for it was Haggai who declared that the Samaritans were unclean, and Haggai who encouraged Zerubbabel on the same day by promising him the Messiahship.

The part of the priests is worthy of careful notice. Haggai (ii. 10–14) says that he asked the priests whether holiness could be communicated by touch and they answered in the negative. Mitchell, in his comment on this passage, says that the stress was laid on the secondary nature of the touching: the holy flesh touches the skirt; the skirt touches food; will the food become holy? a corpse comes in contact with a man; the man touches food; will the food become unclean? And so in the interpretation: the ruined temple makes the Jews unclean; the unclean Jews make their agricultural labours unclean. A parallel is certainly obtained in this way, but it is doubtful whether it was intended by the writer, who does not seem to lay any stress on the secondary nature of the touching. He simply described what was most likely to happen: it was quite likely that the man's skirt or his hand should accidentally touch a dish of food, but very unlikely that the holy flesh itself or a corpse should touch a dish of food. The prophet merely suggested a contingency which was likely to

arise. One might as well say that the question was
of tertiary touching, because a man's skirt was not
likely to touch the actual wine or oil, but only the
skin or jar in which it was kept! There can be little
serious doubt that Haggai's question was equivalent
to asking whether holiness and uncleanness were communicated by touch, and that the priests' reply was
that uncleanness could be communicated by touch,
but that holiness could not. It may further be as-
sumed that the priests in giving this answer were fully
aware of the meaning of Haggai's question, and that
their decision was influenced by the case in point,
i.e. the Samaritans. The unclean Samaritans come to
the holy temple to build, and later on to sacrifice
there. Will the Samaritans become holy or the
temple unclean by the contact?[1] Haggai's comment
(ii. 14) on the priests' reply makes it perfectly plain
that this was the matter under discussion. He says
that the work of their hands (*i.e.* in building the temple), and the sacrifices that they would offer there,
are unclean. Commentators who refer the 'work of
their hands' to agricultural labour seem to have forgotten the word 'there': the sacrifices are offered in the
same place where the work is done. This interpretation shows the meaning of the double decision
that the uncleanness is communicated but the holiness
is not. Under the ordinary interpretation no use was
made by Haggai of the priests' first reply that holiness
was not communicated, as van Hoonacker admits,
"Dans l'application qu'Aggée fait au peuple...il ne

---

[1] The same question was raised in a practical way by our Lord when
He *touched* the leper, with the result that we all know (Mk. i. 41).

met en œuvre que la solution donnée à la seconde
des deux questions." This 'torah' or decision of the
priests would surprise us very much if we did not
know that it was adapted to these special circumstances, for according to the Jewish law it was a false
torah. From the earliest times both holiness and
uncleanness had been regarded as contagious[1], and
this was still held to be true at the time when the
Pentateuch was published, which was certainly later
than Haggai. Uncleanness was of course universally
regarded as contagious, but that holiness was also
contagious was taught in Lev. vi. 20, 21 (E.V. 27, 28)
in the law of the sin offering, "Whatsoever shall touch
the flesh thereof shall be holy; and when there is
sprinkled of the blood thereof on any garment, thou
shalt wash that whereon it was sprinkled in a holy
place. But the earthen vessel wherein it is sodden
shall be broken; and if it be sodden in a brazen vessel, it shall be scoured and rinsed in water." The
command to wash the garment in a holy place was
given because the holiness would be imparted, in a
secondary sense, to the water used in washing, and
in a tertiary sense to the ground where the water was
emptied. The decision of the priests in answer to
Haggai was apparently in direct contradiction to the
law of the sin-offering, and the conclusion must be
drawn that the decision was made for the occasion,
in order that the Samaritans might be rejected. It
was the special business of the priests to give correct
decisions about clean and unclean things, and this was
not the first time that they had been known to give a

---

[1] See W. R. Smith, *Religion of the Semites*, pp. 450 ff.

false torah. Ezekiel, quoting from the earlier prophecy of Zeph. iii. 4, had accused the priests of doing
violence to the torah: "Her priests have done violence to my law...they have put no difference between
the holy and the common, neither have they caused
men to discern between the unclean and the clean,"
Ezek. xxii. 26. It may be, as van Hoonacker says,
that Haggai did not actually put the question to the
priests, but that question and answer are for dramatic
effect; but even so, it is not likely that Haggai would
put into the priests' mouths an answer of which they
would not approve.

Even Zechariah the prophet seems to have stood
on the same side of those who rejected the Samaritans,
for though he echoed Deutero-Isaiah in word, by
speaking of ten men of the Gentiles seizing the skirt
of a Jew saying, "We will go with you, for we have
heard that God is with you" (Zech. viii. 23), yet it
seems that he postponed this sort of thing till the
Messianic days, and his immediate policy was exem-
plified by his treatment of the Samaritan deputation
from Bethel.

The prophets, the priests, the high priest, the civil
governor, and the heads of fathers' houses, with one
accord refused to allow the Samaritans to seek Yahweh, refused to be a light to lighten even their nearest
kinsmen. This unanimous decision was the beginning
of Israel's refusal to be the Servant of the Lord.

With this ends the first Act of the beginnings of
Judaism, and history is a blank for nearly seventy
years until the building of the city walls.

CHAPTER VI

THE FIRST ACT OF JUDAISM[1]

Haggai, the prophet ⎫
Zechariah, the prophet ⎬ leaders of the project to build the temple
Jeshua, the high priest ⎭
The Priests
Zerubbabel, Governor of Judah
Tattenai, Governor Beyond the River
A Samaritan Prophet of Yahweh
A Deputation of Yahweh-worshippers from Bethel
A Psalmist of the Guild of Asaph
Deutero-Isaiah, an aged prophet from Babylon
Jews ⎫ 'the people of the land'
Samaritans ⎭
Heathen, or 'the peoples of the land'
Levites, Singers, Porters, Nethinim, etc.

Scene: Jerusalem.

Time: Beginning in the 6th month of the 2nd year of
Darius I (520 B.C.).

B.C. 520. 6th mo. 1st day.

People of the land: The time has not yet come to build
the temple of Yahweh. Hag. i. 2.

Haggai: Is it a time for you yourselves to dwell in your
panelled houses, while this house lieth waste?... Hag. i. 4.

Go up to the mountain and bring wood and build the
house; and I will take pleasure in it, and I will be glorified,

---

[1] This is not an attempt to write drama, but merely a summary of
the conclusions of the foregoing chapters. In the case of the longer
speeches only the salient verses are given.

saith Yahweh. Ye looked for much, and lo, it came to little; and when ye brought it home I blew upon it. Why? saith Yahweh Sabaoth. Because of my house that lieth waste, while ye run every man to his own house. Therefore on account of you the heavens withhold their dew, and the earth withholds her fruit. And I called for a drought upon the land, and upon the mountains, and upon the corn, and upon the wine, and upon the oil, and upon that which the ground bringeth forth, and upon men, and upon cattle, and upon all the labour of the hands. Hag. i. 8–11.

And now consider, I pray you, from this day and onwards, from before the laying of one stone upon another in the temple of Yahweh, how ye fare. One cometh to a heap of twenty measures and there are ten; one cometh to the wine vat to draw fifty vessels, and there are twenty. Consider: Is the grain still in the barn? Moreover the vine, the fig tree, the pomegranate and the olive tree have not yet borne fruit. From this day will I bless. Hag. ii. 15–19.

6th mo.   24th day.

(*Zerubbabel, Jeshua, and the people of the land began the work.*) Hag. i. 14, 15.

8th mo.   ? 1st day.

Zechariah: Thus saith Yahweh Sabaoth, Return unto me and I will return unto you. Zech. i. 3.

The Samaritans: Let us build with you, for we seek your God as ye do. Ezr. iv. 2.

9th mo.   24th day.

Haggai (*addressing the priests*): If one bear holy flesh in the skirt of his garment, and with his skirt touch bread or pottage or wine or oil or any meat, does it become holy? Hag. ii. 12.

Priests: No.

Haggai: If one that is unclean by a dead body touch any of these does it become unclean? Hag. ii. 13.

Priests: Yes, it does.

Haggai (pointing scornfully at the Samaritans): So is this people, and so is this nation before me, saith Yahweh, and so is every work of their hands, and what they will offer there is unclean. Hag. ii. 14.

Priests: Let Yahweh be glorified! Is. lxvi. 5.

Haggai (aside to Zerubbabel): Thus saith Yahweh, I will shake the heavens and the earth; and I will overthrow the throne of kingdoms, and I will destroy the strength of the kingdoms of the nations; and I will overthrow the chariots, and those that ride in them; and the horses and their riders shall come down, every one by the sword of his brother. In that day, saith Yahweh Sabaoth, I will take thee, O Zerubbabel, my Servant, the son of Shealtiel, and will make thee as a signet; for I have chosen thee. Hag. ii. 21–23.

Zerubbabel, Jeshua, and leading Jews (addressing the Samaritans): Ye have nothing to do with us to build a house unto our God, but we ourselves together will build unto Yahweh, the God of Israel, as king Cyrus, the king of Persia, hath commanded us. Ezr. iv. 3.

(The less devout Samaritans were very angry, and hired counsellors, who laid accusations against the Jews before Tattenai.) Ezr. iv. 5.

Tattenai: Who gave you a decree to build this house and to finish this wall? Ezr. v. 9.

Zerubbabel, Jeshua, and the Jews: We are the servants of the God of heaven and earth, and are building the house that was built these many years ago, which a great king of Israel built and finished. But after our fathers had provoked the God of heaven unto wrath, he gave them into the hand of Nebuchadnezzar king of Babylon, the Chaldean, who destroyed this house, and carried the people away into Babylon. But in the first year of Cyrus king of Babylon, Cyrus the king made a decree to build this house of God. Ezr. v. 11-13.

Tattenai (writes to Darius): Now therefore if it seem good to the king, let search be made in the king's treasure houses, which are there in Babylon, whether it be true that a decree was made by Cyrus the king to build this house of God at Jerusalem, and let the king send his pleasure to us concerning this matter. Ezr. v. 17.

(During the interval that elapses before Tattenai receives a reply from Darius, a Samaritan prophet comes on the scene.)

Samaritan Prophet: I will make mention of the loving-kindnesses of Yahweh, and the praises of Yahweh, according to all that Yahweh hath bestowed on us; and the great goodness toward the house of Israel, which he hath bestowed on them according to his mercies and according to the multitude of his lovingkindnesses. And he said, Surely they are my people, children that will not deal falsely. And he became to them a Saviour in all their affliction. Not an ambassador nor a messenger, but his Presence saved them. In his love and in his pity he redeemed them.... Is. lxiii. 7-9.

Look down from heaven and behold, from the high dwelling of thy holiness and of thy glory. Where are thy zeal and thy mighty acts? Restrain not the yearning of thy bowels and thy tender mercies. For thou art our Father, for Abraham knoweth us not, and Israel doth not acknowledge us; thou Yahweh art our Father, our Redeemer from everlasting is thy name. O Yahweh, why dost thou make us to err from thy ways, and hardenest our heart from fearing thee? Return for the sake of thy servants, for the sake of the tribes of thine inheritance. Why do the wicked march over thy Holy Place, and our adversaries trample thy Sanctuary? We have become those over whom thou hast not ruled from all time, those on whom thy name hath not been named. Oh that thou wouldst rend the heavens and come down, that the mountains might flow down at thy presence!... Is. lxiii. 15–19 (E.V. lxiii. 15–lxiv. 1).

And we have all become as one that is unclean, and all our righteous acts are as a polluted garment; and we all fade as a leaf; and our iniquities as the wind take us away. And there is none that calleth upon thy name, that stirreth up himself to take hold of thee; for thou hast hidden thy face from us, and thou hast delivered us up into the power of our iniquities. But now, O Yahweh, thou art our Father; we are the clay, and thou our potter; and we all are the work of thy hand. Be not wroth very sore, O Yahweh, neither remember iniquity for ever: behold, look, we beseech thee, we are all thy people. Thy holy cities have become a wilderness, Zion hath become a wilderness, Jerusalem a desolation. Our holy and our beautiful House, where our fathers praised thee, is burned with fire, and all our sacred spots are laid waste. Wilt thou refrain thyself for these things, O Yahweh? Wilt thou hold thy peace, and afflict us very sore? Is. lxiv. 5–11 (E.V. lxiv. 6–12).

A Psalmist of the Guild of Asaph (sings):

Give ear, O Shepherd of Israel,
Thou that leadest Joseph like a flock;
Thou that sittest upon the cherubim shine forth.
Before Ephraim and Manasseh
Stir up thy might,
And come to save us.
Turn us again, O God of Hosts,
And cause thy face to shine, that we may be saved.

Ps. lxxx. 2–4 (E.V. 1–3).

(A letter is brought to Tattenai by a messenger from Darius.)

Tattenai (reading): Memorandum. In the first year of Cyrus the king, Cyrus the king made a decree: Concerning the House of God at Jerusalem, let the house be built, the place where they offer sacrifices, and let the foundations thereof be strongly laid.... Ezr. vi. 3.

Now therefore Tattenai, etc., be ye far from thence. Let the work of this House of God alone. Let the Governor of the Jews and the elders of the Jews build this House of God in its place. Ezr. vi. 6, 7.

[*Exit Tattenai.* Ezr. vi. 13.

(Enter a deputation from Bethel.)

B.C. 518. 9th mo. 4th day.

The Deputation: Should I weep in the fifth month (to commemorate the captivity of Judah), separating myself, as I have done these so many years? Zech. vii. 3.

Zechariah (addressing all present): When ye fasted and mourned in the fifth and in the seventh month, even these seventy years, did ye at all fast unto me, even to me? And when ye eat and when ye drink, do ye not eat for yourselves and drink for yourselves.... Zech. vii. 5, 6.

Thus hath Yahweh Sabaoth spoken, saying, Execute true judgment, and show mercy and compassion every man to his brother; and oppress not the widow, nor the fatherless, the stranger, nor the poor; and let none of you imagine evil against his brother in your heart.... Zech. vii. 9, 10.

And it came to pass that, as he cried, and they would not hear; so they shall cry and I will not hear, saith Yahweh Sabaoth. And he scattered them with a whirlwind among all the nations whom they have not known. Thus the land was desolate after them, so that no man passed through nor returned; for they laid the pleasant land desolate. Zech. vii. 13, 14.

Thus saith Yahweh Sabaoth: I am jealous for Zion with great jealousy, and I am jealous for her with great fury. Thus saith Yahweh, I have returned unto Zion and will dwell in the midst of Jerusalem, and Jerusalem shall be called 'The city of Truth,' and the mountain of Yahweh Sabaoth 'The holy mountain.' There shall yet dwell old men and old women in the streets of Jerusalem, each with his staff in his hand for very age. And the streets of the city shall be full of boys and girls playing in the streets thereof. If it be marvellous in the eyes of the remnant of this people in those days, should it also be marvellous in mine eyes? Behold, I will save my people from the land of the rising sun, and from the land of the setting sun; and I will bring them, and they shall dwell in the midst of Jerusalem; and they shall be my people, and I will be their God, in truth and in righteousness.... Zech. viii. 2–8.

Thus saith Yahweh Sabaoth: The fast of the fourth month, and the fast of the fifth, and the fast of the seventh, and the fast of the tenth, shall be to the house of Judah joy and gladness and cheerful feasts. Therefore love truth and peace. Thus saith Yahweh Sabaoth, There shall yet come peoples and inhabitants of many cities; and the inhabitants of one city shall go to another, saying, "Let us by all means go to intreat the favour of Yahweh, and to seek Yahweh Sabaoth," "I will go also." Many peoples and mighty nations shall come to seek Yahweh Sabaoth in Jerusalem, and to intreat the favour of Yahweh. Thus saith Yahweh Sabaoth, In those days ten men of all the tongues of the nations shall seize the skirt of him that is a Jew, saying, "We will go with you, for we have heard that God is with you." Zech. viii. 19–23.

(*Confused noise of heathen without.*)

Deutero-Isaiah (*addressing the idolaters*): I am ready to be enquired of by those who asked not for me; I am ready to be found by those who sought me not. I said, Here am

I, Here am I. unto a nation that hath not called on my name. I have spread out my hands all the day unto a rebellious people, who walk in a way that is not good, after their own thoughts; a people that provoketh me to my face continually, sacrificing in gardens, and burning incense upon bricks; who sit among the graves, and pass the night in the secret places; who eat swine's flesh, and broth of abominable things is in their vessels; who say, "Stand by thyself, come not near to me lest I sanctify thee." These are a smoke in my nose, a fire that burneth all the day.... Is. lxv. 1–5.

(*Addressing Yahweh-worshippers*): Thus saith Yahweh, As the new wine is found in the cluster, and one saith "Destroy it not for a blessing is in it," so will I do for my servants' sakes, that I may not destroy them all. And I will bring forth a seed out of Jacob, and out of Judah an inheritor of my mountains; and my chosen shall inherit it, and my servants shall dwell there.... Is. lxv. 8, 9.

(*Addressing the idolaters*): But ye that forsake Yahweh, that forget my holy mountain, that prepare a table for Gad, and that fill up mingled wine unto Meni; I will destine you to the sword, and ye shall all bow down to the slaughter; because when I called ye did not answer, when I spake ye did not hear; but ye did that which was evil in mine eyes, and chose that wherein I delighted not.... Is. lxv. 11, 12.

And ye shall leave your name for a curse unto my chosen, and the Lord Yahweh shall slay thee; and he shall call his servants by another name; so that he who blesseth himself in the earth shall bless himself in the God of Truth, and he that sweareth in the earth shall swear by the God of Truth, because the former ₐoubles are forgotten, and because they are hid from mine eyes. Is. lxv. 15, 16.

(*Addressing Yahweh-worshippers*): For, behold, I create new heavens and a new earth; and the former things shall not be remembered, nor come into mind. But be ye glad and rejoice for ever over that which I create, for, behold, I create Jerusalem a rejoicing and her people a joy. And I will rejoice in Jerusalem, and joy in my people; and the voice of weeping shall be no more heard in her, nor the voice of crying.... Is. lxv. 17-19.

The wolf and the lamb shall feed together, and the lion shall eat straw like the ox, and dust shall be the serpent's meat. They shall not hurt nor destroy in all my holy mountain, saith Yahweh. Is. lxv. 25.

(*Addressing Haggai, Jeshua, and Zerubbabel*): Thus saith Yahweh, The heaven is my throne, and the earth the footstool of my feet. Where is the house that ye will build me, and where is the sanctuary that shall be my resting place? And all these things, my hand made them, and so all these things came into being, saith Yahweh. But to this one will I look, even to the poor and contrite of spirit, and that trembleth at my word. Killing an ox: slaying a man. Sacrificing a sheep: breaking a dog's neck. Offering an oblation: pouring out swine's blood. Burning frankincense: blessing an idol. Just as they have chosen their ways, and their soul delighteth in their abominations, so will I choose their delusions, and will bring their fears upon them; because when I called no one answered, when I spake they did not hear; but they did that which was evil in mine eyes, and chose that wherein I delighted not. Is. lxvi. 1-4.

(*Addressing the Samaritan Yahweh-worshippers*): Hear the word of Yahweh, ye that tremble at his word: "Your brethren that hate you, that cast you out for my name's sake, have said, 'Let Yahweh be glorified, that we may see your joy,' but they shall be ashamed." A voice of tumult from the city! A voice from the temple! A voice of Yahweh rendering recompence to his enemies!... Is. lxvi. 5, 6.

Rejoice ye with Jerusalem, and be glad for her, all ye that love her. Rejoice for joy with her, all ye that mourn over her; that ye may suck and be satisfied with the breasts of her consolations; that ye may drain out, and be delighted with the abundance of her glory. For thus saith Yahweh, Behold, I will extend peace to her like a river, and the glory of the nations like an overflowing stream. Her children shall be borne upon the side, and shall be dandled upon the knees. As one whom his mother comforteth, so will I comfort you; and ye shall be comforted in Jerusalem. And ye shall see it, and your heart shall rejoice, and your bones shall flourish like the tender grass; and the hand of Yahweh shall be known towards his servants, and he will have indignation against his enemies.... Is. lxvi. 10–14.

(*Addressing all present*): ...to gather together all the nations and the tongues; and they shall come, and they shall see my glory. And I will set on them a sign, and those of them who escape I will send unto the nations, to Tarshish, Pul, and Lud, Meshech, and to Tubal, and Javan, to the distant coasts that have not heard my fame nor seen my glory; and they shall declare my glory among the nations. And they shall bring all your brethren out of all the nations for an offering to Yahweh, upon horses, and in chariots, and in litters, and upon mules, and upon swift beasts, unto my holy mountain Jerusalem, saith Yahweh, as the children of Israel bring the offering in a clean vessel unto the house of Yahweh. And of them also will I take for priests and for Levites, saith Yahweh. For as the new heavens and the new earth, which I will make, shall remain before me, saith Yahweh, so shall your seed and your name remain. Is. lxvi. 18–22.

? B.C. 516. 12th mo. 3rd day.
(*The house was finished.*) Ezr. vi. 15.

B.C. 515. 1st. mo. 14th day.
(*The Passover was celebrated.*) Ezr. vi. 19.

[*Exeunt the heathen.* Ezr. vi. 21.

CHAPTER VII

ZERUBBABEL TO NEHEMIAH

THE building of the temple at Jerusalem was a great achievement. Nothing but religious zeal could have brought it about. Encouragement certainly came from Babylonia to perform the work, but we have no reason to suppose that it was financed from that quarter or by wealthy Jews who had returned. The story, as we have seen it, gives the impression of Judaean farmers, just beginning to earn a little more than was necessary for immediate needs, being stirred by Haggai to a pitch of enthusiasm, and investing their little savings in the building of the temple. Their religious devotion cost them heavily. The restored temple was no doubt an incentive to religious development, and especially to the development of the cultus; but the people's savings were gone, and this rather large expenditure had exhausted so much of their capital that the Restoration in a worldly sense was seriously checked. Seventy years had to elapse before the rebuilding of the city was successfully taken in hand by Nehemiah. Our history book, Ezra and Nehemiah, has nothing to say about this long period, till one incident quite at its close; but the period was by no means unimportant, for when the nation emerges again into the light under Nehemiah we see a much more organized and settled state of society.

The most important literature belonging to the period is to be found in the book of Isaiah. Some have regarded the later chapters as all the work of one man Trito-Isaiah, while others have regarded them as a collection of writings of different authors. We have already disposed of lxiii. 7–lxvi., and we are therefore left to consider the remainder. The attempt is here made to show that the four sections xlix. 14–l. 3, lviii.–lix., lx.–lxii., lxiii. 1–6, are the work of one hand, and betray themselves as such by numerous parallelisms of thought and words. It will be best to begin with the verses that speak of the ruined walls and other desolations and the hopes of restoration, because they prove that the sections were written before the time of Nehemiah.

xlix. 16, 17. "Behold I have graven thee upon the palms of my hands; thy walls are continually before me. Thy children make haste; thy destroyers and they that made thee waste shall go forth from thee." [For 'thy children' בָּנַיִךְ we should perhaps read 'thy builders' בֹּנַיִךְ which is supported by the versions. Duhm and Marti want to emend further on grounds of metre.]

xlix. 19 a. "For, as for thy waste and thy desolate places and thy land that hath been destroyed—"

lviii. 12. "And those that are of thee [מִמְּךָ; perhaps read בָּנַיִךְ 'thy children' (Weir, Cheyne)] shall build the old waste places; thou shalt raise up the foundations of many generations; and thou shalt be called The Repairer of the Breach, the Restorer of paths for dwelling."

lx. 10. "And strangers shall build thy walls."

lx. 11. "Thy gates also shall be open continually; they shall not be shut day nor night."

lx. 18. "Thou shalt call thy walls salvation and thy gates praise."

lxi. 4. "And they shall build the old wastes, they shall raise up the former desolations, and they shall repair the waste cities, the desolations of many generations."

lxii. 3. "And thou (Zion) shalt be a crown of beauty in the hand of Yahweh, and a royal diadem in the hand of thy God."

lxii. 5. "For as a young man marrieth a virgin, so shall thy Builder marry thee" [reading יִבְעָלֵךְ בֹּנֵךְ].

lxii. 6, 7. "I have set watchmen upon thy walls, O Jerusalem; they shall never hold their peace day nor night. Ye that are Yahweh's remembrancers, take ye no rest, and give Him no rest, till He establish and till He make Jerusalem a praise in the earth."

lxii. 12. "And thou shalt be called Sought-out, Unforsaken City."

It will be noticed that the greater number of these references, and the more definite ones, come from lx.–lxii., from which it may be inferred that the restoration of the walls was becoming practical politics at the time when those chapters were written. There is a very clearly marked contrast with the fairy city depicted in liv. 11, 12 which could not have been written at a time when men were seriously considering plans for building the city:—

"Behold I will lay thy stones with stibnite[1],
And I will lay thy foundations with sapphires.
I will make thy pinnacles of rubies,
And thy gates of carbuncles,
And all thy border of precious stones."

xlix. 14–26 shows further parallels with lx.–lxii. :—

xlix. 18; lx. 4. "Lift up thine eyes round about and see. All of them gather themselves together; they come unto thee" (verbally identical).

xlix. 26; lx. 16. "That I Yahweh am thy saviour, and thy redeemer, the Mighty One of Jacob" (verbally identical).

xlix. 18. "As I live, saith Yahweh, thou shalt surely clothe thee with them all as with an ornament, and gird thyself with them like a bride."

lxi. 10. "For He hath clothed me with the garments of salvation; He hath covered me with the robe of righteousness, as a bridegroom prepareth (reading יְכִין for יְכַהֵן) his turban, and as a bride adorneth herself with her jewels."

xlix. 22. "And they shall bring thy sons in their bosom, and thy daughters shall be carried upon their shoulder."

lx. 4. "Thy sons shall come from far, and thy daughters shall be nursed upon the side."

---

[1] Commentators do not know the beauty of stibnite, and want to emend the word. Stibnite is antimony sulphide, which occurs in nature as black prismatic crystals, sometimes of great size. That it was known to the Jews in this form is proved by the name 'Keren-happuch,' '*horn* of stibnite,' (Job xlii. 14). Commentators have usually thought of the crushed commercial article, an impalpable powder, with which the eastern ladies used to darken their eyes.

xlix. 23. "And kings shall be thy nursing fathers, and their queens thy nursing mothers. They shall bow down to thee with their faces to the earth, and shall lick the dust of thy feet."

lx. 16. "And thou shalt suck the breast of kings."

lx. 14. "And the sons of them that afflicted thee shall come bending unto thee,[and all they that despised thee shall bow themselves down at the soles of thy feet][1]."

The first two of the above parallels where the wording is identical appear to be in context in both positions. It is not therefore a question of later interpolation. The author of one must have copied the other, or if he was the same author he simply repeated himself. The other three parallels are good evidence for unity of authorship, for the wording is dissimilar and yet the ideas are the same. xlix. 23 *a* is so foreign to the thought of Deutero-Isaiah that Duhm and Marti both wish to treat it as a later interpolation. Marti mentions the fact that it harmonizes better with the pride of later Judaism,. and he compares lx. 10, 16, lxi. 5. It is a question whether it is any more arbitrary to cut out the whole section xlix. 14–26 from its present context than the single half verse 23 *a*. Further, the references to rebuilding the walls point to the same occasion for xlix. 14–26 and lx.–lxii.; and we can therefore conclude that the two sections are the work of one author, and were written about the same time.

l. 1–3 is usually taken with xlix. 22–26, as forming together three short oracles. But parallels to l. 1–3 are to be found rather with lix. than with lx.–lxii.:—

[1] Omitted by the Hexaplaric Greek.

l. 1. "Behold for your iniquities were ye sold, and for your transgressions was your mother put away."

lix. 2. "But your iniquities have separated between you and your God, and your sins have hid His face from you that He will not hear."

l. 2. "Why, when I came, was there no man? when I called was there none to answer? Is my hand indeed shortened, that it cannot redeem? or have I no power to deliver?"

lix. 16. "And He saw that there was no man, and wondered that there was no intercessor."

lix. 1. "Behold, Yahweh's hand is not shortened that it cannot save; nor His ear heavy that it cannot hear."

l. 1–3 is too short a section for one to be able to speak confidently of its authorship, but these parallels would certainly suggest connexion with lix., while the metrical arrangement suggests connexion with xlix. 22–26, and therefore with the author of lx.–lxii. The question immediately arises whether lviii.–lix. and lx.–lxii. are by the same author. The tone of the two is very different, the former wearing a gloomy aspect and the latter a cheerful one, but this could be sufficiently accounted for by some change in external conditions which took place before lx.–lxii. was written. The author of lviii., lix. was not without hope, in spite of his gloom, and he ends up with the new covenant of the Spirit:—

lix. 21. "And as for me, this is my covenant with them, saith Yahweh: My Spirit that is upon thee, and my words which I have put in thy mouth, shall not depart out of thy mouth..."

This is clearly parallel to the opening of chapter lxi.:—

lxi. 1. "The Spirit of the Lord Yahweh is upon me,
        Because Yahweh hath anointed me.
        To preach good tidings to the meek He
            hath sent me,
        To bind up the broken-hearted..."

Both these are dependent on Deutero-Isaiah's description of the Servant of the Lord, cf. li. 16 "I have put my words in thy mouth," xlii. 1 "I have put my Spirit upon him," and xlii. 7. Besides this there are the following parallels between lviii., lix. and lx.–lxii.:—

lviii. 8. "Then shall thy light break forth as the morning."

lviii. 10. "And thy light shall rise in the darkness, and thine obscurity shall be as the noonday."

lix. 9, 10. "We look for light, but lo, darkness! for brightness, but we walk in obscurity...we stumble at noonday as in the twilight."

lx. 1. "Arise, shine, for thy light is come!"

lix. 21. "This is my covenant with them...from henceforth and for ever."

lxi. 8. "I will make an everlasting covenant with them."

lviii. 12, and lxi. 4, the reference to the restoration of the old waste places, already quoted.

In lxiii. 1–6 we have the link which completes the connexion between the different passages under consideration:—

lxiii. 5. "And I looked, and there was none to help, and I wondered that there was none to uphold. Therefore mine own arm brought salvation unto me, and my fury upheld me."

lix. 16. "And he saw that there was no man, and he wondered that there was no intercessor. Therefore his own arm brought salvation unto him, and his righteousness upheld him."

Of these verses Marti says, "One is obliged to admit that the author himself repeats himself." It is true that li. 18 is also parallel in thought, but on grounds of metre and context it is regarded by Duhm, Marti, and others as an interpolated verse in its present position. lix. 17, 18 is akin to lxiii. 1–6 in its idea of Yahweh's vengeance on the heathen. Ewald[1] recognized that lxiii. 1–6 was by the same author as lviii., lix.

lxiii. 6. "And I trod down the people in mine anger, and I made them drunk in my fury, and I poured out their life-blood on the earth."

xlix. 26. "And I will feed them that oppress thee with their own flesh, and they shall be drunken with their own blood as with sweet wine."

From the foregoing parallels we can conclude that the author of xlix. 14–26 and lx.–lxii. also wrote l. 1–3, lviii.–lix., and lxiii. 1–6, though not necessarily all at the same time. For the sake of convenience we shall speak of the author of these sections as Trito-Isaiah.

Three references in lx.–lxii. show that the temple was standing, and the intention at that time was to make it more magnificent:—

[1] Quoted by Cheyne on Isaiah lxiii. 1–6.

lx. 7. "And I will beautify my beautiful house."

lx. 13. "The glory of the Lebanon shall come unto
thee,

The fir-tree, the pine, and the box-tree together,

To beautify the place of my sanctuary."

lxii. 9. "And they that have gathered it shall drink
it in the courts of my sanctuary."

Such things could have been written at any time
after the temple was built, and the references to beautifying it are in such an apocalyptic setting that they
need not necessarily imply any real movement towards
decorating the temple or improving its ritual. But as
a first approximation to the date it is useful to know
that chapters lx.–lxii. were written after 515 and before
444 B.C. The other sections dealt with, being by the
same author, will probably fall within the same period.

Before going further it should be noticed that
other cities needed rebuilding besides Jerusalem (lxi. 4,
cf. lxiv. 9 (E.V. 10), Zech. i. 12, vii. 7); but it is the
building of Jerusalem which appears nearest to the
heart of God, and it is to be accomplished as a mark
of favour towards His people. The renewed walls will
be a sign of His salvation and the gates will declare
His praise (lx. 18). The prophet evidently wishes to
guard against the notion of military aggression in this
work: the walls are not aggression but salvation, and
the gates will be open continually.

Both lxi. 4 and lviii. 12 speak of the desolation as
something ancient. When we come to Nehemiah however we seem to be in the face of a recent tragedy.

Neh. i. 3 says, "the wall of Jerusalem is breached (מְפֹרָצֶת), and its gates have been burnt (נִצְּתוּ) with fire," ii. 3 "the city, the place of my fathers' sepulchres, lieth waste (חֲרֵבָה) and its gates have been consumed (אֻכְּלוּ) by fire," ii. 13 "the walls of Jerusalem which are breached (פְּרוּצִים, Kethib perhaps הַמְפֹרָצִים) and its gates have been consumed (אֻכְּלוּ) by fire," ii. 17 "Jerusalem lieth waste (חֲרֵבָה) and its gates have been burnt (נִצְּתוּ) with fire." The grammar is instructive: the city and the walls are described by the condition in which they lie, expressed by a participle or adjective; the gates are spoken of as having suffered a calamity, expressed by the perfect. The conclusion is that the burning of the gates at any rate was a recent event, while as far as the grammar goes the destruction of the walls might be ancient or recent. But in addition to this evidence, Nehemiah's outburst of grief on hearing the news shows that the condition of Jerusalem was partly, if not wholly, due to some new calamity.

It is necessary therefore to suppose that between the writing of Is. lx.–lxii. and the time of Nehemiah's visit, some attempt had been made to restore the ruins of Jerusalem. Gates had been set up, as Nehemiah specially refers to the fact of their having been burnt, and some work more or less had probably been done on the walls. The walls however had not been completed, and that is why their condition was described as we have seen: they had never quite ceased to be the ruins in which they had lain these many years.

With this indirect evidence suggesting an attempted restoration of the city, it is only a perverse criticism that can fail to see a narrative of the event in Ezr. iv. 7–23. In that chapter there is a record of how the Jews began to build and how they were frustrated "by force and power." The incident is related to have happened in the reign of Artaxerxes who came to the throne in 464 B.C. Nehemiah learnt the news in 445, probably soon after the event. If we are right in surmising that Is. lx.–lxii. was the immediate cause of the attempt at restoration, it was probably written in the neighbourhood of 450, and certainly between the limits of 465 and 445 B.C. This close approximation to the exact date is of some considerable value to us, as the religious and political ideas of the section are characteristic. xlix. 14–l. 3 will probably have been written somewhere about the same time, and lviii., lix., lxiii. 1–6 a little earlier. But for our immediate historical purpose the most important thing is to have settled the date of lx.–lxii.

The outlook of Trito-Isaiah is different from that of Deutero-Isaiah. It is true that Deutero-Isaiah had contemplated the return of Jews from other places besides Babylonia (xliii. 5, 6, xlix. 12), but it was Babylon to which his gaze was mainly directed (see especially xlviii. 20). But Trito-Isaiah had fixed his gaze on the Great Sea in the West. From Arabia (Midian, Ephah, Sheba, Kedar, Nebaioth) he expected the Gentiles to bring their wealth; but no return of Jews was expected from there, and no mention is made of Babylon at all. His main interest was in the return of Jews laden with the fabled wealth of distant islands[1]: "For the abundance of the sea shall be turned unto thee; the wealth of the nations shall come unto thee," lx. 5; "Surely the ships shall gather together unto me [reading צִיִּים יְקַוּוּ] with the ships of Tarshish in the van, to bring thy sons from far, their silver and their gold with them," lx. 9; "Thou shalt suck the milk of nations and shalt suck the breast of kings," lx. 16; "Ye shall eat the wealth of nations, and in their glory ye shall boast yourselves," lxi. 6. The last quotation but one seems almost to be a deliberate contradiction of the hope expressed in lxvi. 10, 11 in which the friends of Jerusalem are invited to rejoice in her prosperity, "that ye may suck and be satisfied with the breasts of her consolations; that ye may drain out and be delighted with the abundance of her glory." The whole idea of the exploitation of the Gentiles for the benefit of the Jews is foreign to the thought of Deutero-Isaiah. We remember the universalistic hopes held by him, and especially the task on behalf of the Gentiles entrusted to the Servant of the Lord. Here we find that even when Trito-Isaiah is copying the description of the Servant (lxi. 1, 2) he omits all reference to the mission to the Gentiles. At first sight lx. 3 "Nations shall come to thy light, and kings to the brightness of thy rising" might be thought to embody the idea. But read in its context it suggests more the idea of a lamp with its fatal attraction for moths than the idea of a

---

[1] The question whether the silver and gold belonged to the Jewish exiles or the Gentiles is futile. The Jews were to get it from the Gentiles, but whether by legitimate trading, or in the way that their forefathers 'spoiled the Egyptians' (Ex. xii. 35, 36, Ps. cv. 37), does not really matter.

"light to lighten the Gentiles." The Gentiles are definitely to be subjugated to the Jews, "Strangers shall stand and feed your flocks, and aliens shall be your ploughmen and your vine-dressers," lxi. 5; "Strangers shall build up thy walls, and their kings shall minister unto thee," lx. 10; "Kings shall be thy nursing fathers, and their queens thy nursing mothers; they shall bow down to thee with their faces to the earth and lick the dust of thy feet," xlix. 23. Even vengeance is to be taken on the Gentiles as enemies of Yahweh, "According to their deeds, accordingly He will repay, fury to His adversaries, recompence to His enemies," lix. 18, and the picture of xlix. 26 and lxiii. 1–6 is terrible in its realism. Stress must not be laid in this connexion on lx. 12, 14 $a\beta$, because their interference with the metre shows them to be later additions. The religious rôle to be played by the Gentiles is even more surprising: they are to bring offerings to the temple, gold and frankincense; their flocks will march to Jerusalem and mount the altar; the wood of Lebanon will be given for the temple, and the gold, silver, brass and iron of the nations will be brought in (lx. 6, 7, 13, 17). By such gifts they will declare the praises of the Lord (lx. 6), but the position of religious privilege is not for them, "but ye (the Jews) shall be named the priests of Yahweh, men shall call you the ministers of our God" (lxi. 6). The attitude of intolerance shown towards the Gentiles was natural enough to people who were continually suffering from raids on their crops (lxii. 8), and it must be remembered that we have no evidence of Deutero-Isaiah's aspirations ever being accepted by his contemporaries. Thus Trito-

Isaiah held out no hope of more than a subordinate position for the Gentiles. At the same time he had quite high moral ideas, *e.g.* lviii. 6 "Is not this the fast that I have chosen, to loose the bands of wickedness, to undo the bonds of the yoke, to let the oppressed go free, and that ye break every yoke?" and throughout chapters lviii. and lix. The apocalyptic picture which he paints is distinctly on a moral background, *e.g.* "Violence shall no more be heard in thy land...Yahweh shall be thine everlasting light...thy people also shall be all righteous" (lx. 18–21); "so the Lord Yahweh will cause righteousness and praise to spring forth before all the nations," lxi. 11.

It is rather important to recognize that Trito-Isaiah was acquainted with the work of Deutero-Isaiah. lx. 9 "For the name of Yahweh thy God, and for the Holy One of Israel, for He hath glorified thee" was either copied by the author, or inserted by a later scribe, from lv. 5 which is verbally identical except for the first word. lxi. 1, 2 is, as we have seen, reminiscent of the Servant Poem xlii. 1–7. lxi. 11 is reminiscent of lv. 10, 11. lxii. 5 (emended) "so shall thy Builder marry thee" is similar to liv. 5 "for thy Maker is thy husband, Yahweh Sabaoth is His name." xlix. 18 is perhaps reminiscent of the Servant's task in restoring Israel, xlix. 6. xlix. 25 "I will contend with him that contendeth with thee" refers to l. 8 "He is near that justifieth me. Who will contend with me?" The list is sufficient to show a fair acquaintance with his predecessor's work. We have seen already that he was distinctly inferior to his predecessor in his outlook towards the gentiles, and in the case of lxi. 1 we know

that he deliberately omitted the idea of Israel being a
light to lighten the Gentiles. Now from his high moral
tone Trito-Isaiah must have been a spiritual leader of
Israel in his day, and from his references to the lack
of leaders (lix. 16, lxiii. 5) he was probably the only
great spiritual leader. And yet he deliberately rejected
Deutero-Isaiah's universalistic ideas. This is clear evidence that the history of the post-exilic period is the
history of a decline from a great ideal. Even within
Deutero-Isaiah's lifetime there had been the rejection
of the Samaritans, against which he protested; but
now, some sixty or seventy years later, the doctrine
of love for other nations had been still more obscured,
and Trito-Isaiah, the chief religious leader of the day,
could hold out no better hope for the Gentiles than subjugation to the Jews or the merciless vengeance of the
Lord. This was the atmosphere which made possible,
a little later, the policy of Nehemiah and Ezra of separating the Jews from the 'defilement' of the Gentiles.

We turn now to the account in Ezr. iv. 7–23 of an
attempt to restore the city walls. This is one of the
Aramaic parts of the book of Ezra; and many writers,
while acknowledging that they are not faithful copies
of the original documents, yet believe them to be
based on historical facts. Some would think that the
original documents had been coloured in transmission
and edited, while others would admit them to be free
compositions by an author who chose this form for his
historical material. Torrey regards such an attitude
as altogether unreasonable. He says[1], "When documents lie before us which in form do not appear to be

[1] *Ezra Studies*, p. 142 n.

authentic, whose statements we cannot control from any other source, and of whose author or authors we know nothing, beyond the fact that they obviously write with a 'tendency,' we cannot legitimately make use of them." With regard, however, to Ezr. iv. 7–23 we have seen that we can control the statements from two other sources, for Is. lx.–lxii. shows that there was a stir to build the walls, the gates, and the city, and Neh. i. 3 shows that the gates and probably also the walls had suffered a recent calamity. These two sources compel us to suppose that some work was done towards restoring the city after Is. lx.–lxii. was written, and that shortly before 445 B.C. the city gates had been burnt and probably damage had been done to the walls at the same time. In Ezr. iv. 7–23 we have a record of just such a thing. The opening verses, Ezr. iv. 7–11, I Esdras ii. 15, 16 (E.V. 16, 17), are in much confusion, a discussion of which will be found in Torrey's *Ezra Studies*, pp. 178–183, and in Batten's *Commentary*, pp. 166–169. It is clear that at the least *vv.* 9 *b*, 10 are an interpolation. Verse 17 shows that in the narrative as it originally stood it was Rehum and Shimshai and other people in Samaria who made the complaint, and *v.* 14 "because we eat the salt of the palace" shows that they were in the pay of the Persian court, whatever their nationality may have been. That is, the complaint was a political one made by Persian officials living in Samaria, and not, as the interpolated verses 9, 10 wish us to believe, by the native population whom we know as the Samaritans. The subject of the complaint was merely a political one, that Jerusalem was being rebuilt, and would be a

menace to the peace of the Persian Empire. The
exact wording of the charge (*v.* 12) is that "they are
building the rebellious and bad city; they are completing the walls and laying the foundations." M. T.
has וְשׁוּרַיָ אֶשְׁכְלִלוּ, the Qre having the perfect tense
וְשׁוּרַיָּא שְׁכְלִלוּ "they have completed the walls." But
Torrey points out that this is contradicted by *v.* 13 "if
this city be builded and the walls completed," and that
therefore it must have read an imperfect וְשׁוּרַיָּא
אֶשְׁכְלִלוּ "they are completing the walls." The com-
plainants urged that the king should enquire in the
record books and see how rebellious Jerusalem had
been in the past. The king did so, and replied that
they were to stop the work until further decree from
him. On receiving the letter they stopped the work
by force of arms. It is evident that the letters are not
genuine, *i.e.* not the actual letters that passed; but the
Aramaic writer who composed them was correctly
informed of the main facts of the case, viz. that an
attempt was made before the time of Nehemiah to
rebuild the city and especially the walls, that the
officials at Samaria regarded this as a threat to rebel
and reported the matter to the king, who gave them
authority to stop the work, which they did by force.
Indeed they seem to have done more than stop the
work, for they destroyed the work that was already done.

This was the condition of affairs which was reported
to Nehemiah (Neh. i. 3) "The remnant that are left
of the captivity there in the province[1] are in great

---

[1] The word מדינה 'province' is a general term, and here means the
province of Judah, and not of course the whole of the fifth satrapy. See
below, p. 146.

reproach; the wall of Jerusalem also is broken down
and the gates thereof have been burned with fire.
"The remnant that are left of the captivity" must
mean captive Israelites who had returned to Palestine
from Babylon, and it is quite likely that this abortive
attempt to rebuild the walls was undertaken by a
caravan of exiles who had returned only a short time
previously. This is what is stated by the Aramaic
source, in which the accusers lay the blame for the
building on "the Jews who have come up from thy
country (מִן לְוָתָךְ 'de chez toi')" and who "have come
unto us to Jerusalem," Ezr. iv. 12. What was reported
to Nehemiah was apparently not only the failure of
the enterprise, but the forlorn state of the returned
exiles who had undertaken it.

To this same period, just before the arrival of Nehemiah, probably belongs the short prophecy bearing
the name Malachi. The indications of its date are
very slight. It belongs to the Persian period, when
Judah was under a governor (פחה), Mal. i. 8. The
same verse shows that the governor was not Nehemiah, for Nehemiah never received presents (Neh.
v. 15). The temple had been standing long enough
for its service to be neglected. The prophecy was
written in dark days when people doubted whether
Yahweh cared at all for them. The prophet complains
because the tithes are neglected, and he does so in a
way that fits in well with the action taken later by
Nehemiah and Ezra, and as we shall see later[1] the
method of tithing was exactly the same as that which
was customary in Nehemiah's time. Two questions

[1] P. 195.

relating to marriage are dealt with. First the writer
inveighs against the practice of marrying foreign wives
which yoked the servants of Yahweh with worshippers
of strange gods (Mal. ii. 11, 12), an abuse which
Nehemiah and Ezra took stringent measures to correct. And secondly he complains about the prevalence
of divorce (Mal. ii. 14), suggesting that Jews were
putting away the Jewish wives, whom they had married in their youth, so as to contract these foreign
alliances. Just as Haggai had regarded the misfortunes
of Israel as due to failure to build the temple, so
Malachi regards the neglect of tithes, and the offering
of blemished sacrifices, as the cause of the misfortunes
of his day. If only the sacrifices were duly offered by
a faithful priesthood Yahweh would be pleased with
them (iii. 4), and if only the tithes were given in full
the ground would be more fruitful and Judah would
become a delightsome land (iii. 12). We notice in all
this an extraordinary reliance on the outward forms of
religion, as if it was the due performance of ceremonies
which Yahweh chiefly desired; but this impression is
tempered somewhat by the appeal for justice and the
condemnation of oppression which we find in iii. 5.
Still, Malachi's emphasis on sacrifice and ritual is in
striking contrast with the depreciation of these things
which we find in the earlier prophets; and there is
nothing else in the whole Old Testament comparable
with his conception of the priesthood as the Messenger
or Angel of Yahweh (ii. 7). That term had been used
in earlier writings for the outward form in which
Yahweh appeared when he wished to make his will
known to men. It had never been claimed even by

the prophets, and now it is applied to priests as if the whole will of God was expressed in their ministrations at the altar. A remarkable verse, which has given rise to much comment, is i. 11 where, after having spoken of the unworthy offerings at the temple, he says, "For from the rising of the sun even unto the going down of the same my name is great among the nations; and in every place (or 'sanctuary') smoke is made to arise to my name, even a pure offering." As the offering here referred to is made in the name of Yahweh it cannot be, as some have suggested, that the prophet, in an outburst of universalism regarded the offerings of the heathen to their gods as being acceptable to Yahweh, nor would such a view be in agreement with the writer's estimate of other religions (ii. 11, 12). Rather it means that the Jews of the dispersion, by the purity of their offerings at such sanctuaries as Elephantine and Casiphia, commended the worship of Yahweh among the nations; and this the prophet contrasted with the conduct of the sacrifices at Jerusalem.

CHAPTER VIII

INDEPENDENCE FROM SAMARIA

THE Memoirs of Nehemiah which the Chronicler has incorporated into his work are an historical source of great value. It would be too much to expect that the Chronicler had left them untouched, but even allowing for a certain amount of addition and embellishment there is a sufficient residuum of undoubted history to make us feel that here at any rate we are treading on firm ground. It is not that we are supplied with any wealth of detail as to the conditions of the time or the history of Nehemiah, nor that the text itself is always in a good state of preservation, but what we are told is reliable.

The previous chapter discussed the events which preceded 444 B.C., the futile attempt to restore the city, and the great affliction and reproach that had fallen on the Judaean community. Nehemiah is introduced to us as a cup-bearer to king Artaxerxes I in the castle at the Persian metropolis of Shushan or Susa. It is not clear whether he was the chief butler, or only one of many, and on this would depend our estimate of his position in the kingdom. More probably he was only a subordinate butler, and his position, though one of dignity, would not be that of a high officer of state. From his reference to the graves of his forefathers at Jerusalem (ii. 3) it is quite likely that Nehemiah was of royal Jewish descent, and this would add point to Sanballat's accusation that he was plotting rebellion against king Artaxerxes (ii. 19) and setting himself up as king of Judah (vi. 6, 7). The news of the misfortunes of Judah and Jerusalem was brought to Nehemiah by one of his relatives, perhaps an actual brother, named Hanani, and a party of men recently returned from Judah. Nehemiah was over-whelmed with grief, and passed some days in mourning, fasting and praying. The opportunity of laying the matter before the king came on an occasion when it was his duty to serve the king at table. Fortunately it was a moment when he was in favour with the monarch—following Batten's translation of ii. 1 וְלֹא־הָיִיתִי רַע לְפָנָיו "I was not out of favour with him." Nehemiah's face betrayed the grief of his heart, and the king, noticing it, asked the cause. It was the opportunity for which Nehemiah had been waiting and praying for the last four months. Taking his courage in both hands he declared at once the cause of his trouble, hoping no doubt that the king would forget that it was owing to his own royal decree that the recent building operations had been hindered: "Let the king live for ever! Why should not my countenance be sad, when the city, the place of my fathers' sepulchres, lieth waste, and the gates thereof have been consumed by fire?" (ii. 3). The king made a non-committal reply, "For what dost thou make request?" and Nehemiah, knowing everything de-pended on the king's mood at the moment, offered a silent prayer to God, the gist of which at any rate is recorded in the previous chapter, "Prosper I pray thee thy servant this day and grant him mercy in the sight of this man" (i. 11). Batten is probably correct in thinking that these words have been displaced from their original position after ii. 4. Nehemiah then made his request, not merely for permission of absence, but to be sent on a mission from the king to rebuild Jerusalem. The king enquired how long the whole mission would take, including the time of going and returning, and forthwith granted the request. Nehemiah gives us no account of his journey, except that he was provided with a military escort, and with letters to the various governors "Beyond the River."

From the time of Zerubbabel until Nehemiah we do not know the names of any of the governors of Judah. Neh. v. 15 tells us that there had been at any rate some governors during the interval, but this very statement shows that such men had not worked for the benefit of the Jews—"The former governors that were before me were a burden to the people, and received from them daily [so the Vulgate] forty shekels of silver for bread and wine." They certainly were not looked upon as champions of Jewish rights, as witness the complaint of Trito-Isaiah shortly before Nehemiah's time that there was no one to uphold nor to interpose on behalf of the Jews (Is. lix. 16, lxiii. 5). Nehemiah does not tell us at the beginning of his narrative that he was given the office of governor of Judah, and he only mentions it incidentally in v. 14, where however he makes it plain that he held the office from the time of his arrival—the twentieth year of Artaxerxes[1]. There were apparently a number of Persian governors in Palestine and Syria, for Nehe-

[1] He is also given the title of governor in Neh. xii. 26.

miah had asked for letters to the "governors beyond
the River" (פַּחֲווֹת עֵבֶר הַנָּהָר‎ Neh. ii. 7, 9). We learn
from Herodotus that Darius I had initiated the method
of governing by satraps, and for this purpose the
Persian Empire was divided into twenty satrapies.
The arrangement of the satrapies was occasionally
changed. The fifth one of them as described in Herodotus III. 91, included Phoenicia, Syria or Palestine,
Cyprus, and part of Arabia, which corresponds to
the Aramaic title "Beyond the River," *i.e.* West of
Euphrates. Mazaeus, who was Satrap of Cilicia and
Syria in the time of Darius III and of Alexander, is
described on his coins as "Mazdai who is [placed]
over the country beyond the Euphrates, and Cilicia."
Each satrapy was subdivided into minor governor-
ships, and the governors of these were called satraps
or hyparchs. The word פֶּחָה‎ 'governor' seems also
to have been used broadly for either the higher or the
lower office[1]. Guthe supposes that the seat of the satrap
of the fifth province was at Damascus or Aleppo, and
if so his distance from Jerusalem would explain why
we never read of any interference by him in Judaean
affairs. At the time of Nehemiah, the governor of
Samaria was Sanballat. His name is recorded by
Nehemiah, but it is only through the Elephantine
papyri that we have learnt that he held this office.
Now Sanballat's attitude to Nehemiah suggests very
strongly that the post of governor of Judah had been

---

[1] See Ed. Meyer, art. "Satrap" in *Encyclop. Britannica*, 11th edition;
Prášek, *Geschichte der Meder u. Perser*, vol. II., p. 45 f.; Guthe,
Geschichte des Volkes Israel, ed. i., p. 248, or ed. iii., p. 281; Hölscher,
Palästina, pp. 2, 5.

vacant for a while when Nehemiah arrived, and that
such oversight as was necessary had been left to
Sanballat. This will explain why Sanballat and his
friends were so grieved at Nehemiah's arrival even
before they knew what policy he would adopt (Neh.
ii. 10–12). We are expressly told that they did not
know at this time that he intended to build the walls.
But they knew that his appointment as governor of
Judah would put an end to Sanballat's power there.
As soon as the project for building the walls was
known Sanballat accused Nehemiah of rebelling a-
gainst the Persian king. Such an accusation had held
good previously (Ezr. iv. 12, 13) when unauthorized
persons had tried to restore the walls; and the Samaritan authorities, in the absence of a governor of Judah,
had been able to stop the work. But now the position
was quite different, for the work was being carried out
under the orders of Nehemiah, a Persian governor,
who was not responsible to the governor of Samaria,
but to the king Artaxerxes, and indeed had the king's
written permission for the work. Nehemiah therefore
answered the accusation of Sanballat by serving him
and his associates with a notice to quit, saying that
they had "no property, nor authority, nor proof of
citizenship in Jerusalem" (Neh. ii. 20). There is an
obscure phrase in Neh. iii. 7, which may quite probably refer to an official residence of the Persian
governor in Jerusalem (לְכִסֵּא פַּחַת עֵבֶר הַנָּהָר). The
verse has often been interpreted as meaning that the
satrap of the whole province Beyond the River had
his residence at Mizpah, and mention has been made

of the fact that Gedaliah 140 years previously had
lived at Mizpah. But Gedaliah only went to Mizpah
so as to keep a look out lest the Babylonians should
return, as we are told in Jer. xl. 10, for the name
Mizpah means Watchtower, and if it is to be identified
with Nebi Samwil it commanded a magnificent view.
Moreover Gedaliah was not a satrap, and is never
even described as פֶּחָה. The satraps always lived
in one of the larger towns of their province. It seems
safer therefore to refer this verse to a residence in
Jerusalem, not of the satrap of the whole province,
but of one of the minor governors. If the house had
been occupied by Sanballat on his visits to Jerusalem,
and only deserted when Nehemiah gave him notice to
quit, Nehemiah may not have taken up his residence
there, and this would explain why it is called im-
personally "the throne of the governor beyond the
River," instead of "the throne of Nehemiah" or "the
throne of the governor of Judah."

Sanballat, although such an inveterate enemy to
Nehemiah, and in spite of his Babylonian name,
either was actually an Israelite, or had distinctly
Israelite sympathies; for his two sons, mentioned in
the Elephantine papyri, bore the Israelite names of
Delaiah and Shelemiah. Associated with Sanballat
were two men who were certainly foreigners. The
first was an Ammonite named Tobiah, who bore the
epithet 'Slave,' and the second was Geshem or Gashmu
an Arabian. The name Gashmu is found in Naba-
taean inscriptions. Tobiah's parents, or whoever gave
him his name, could scarcely have chosen a name
more expressive of loyalty to Yahweh than 'Tobiah'

which means "Yahweh is good." We may guess that he was the child of a mixed marriage of an Ammonite and a Jewess. He himself married a Jewess, and obtained a Jewish wife for his son, and thereby had many sworn friends in Judah (Neh. vi. 18). It is even possible that he was related by marriage to Eliashib the high-priest (Neh. xiii. 4), but the expression may not mean more than the alliance of friendship. We shall see later that Sanballat gave his daughter in marriage to one of the Jewish high-priestly family (Neh. xiii. 28). From these facts we may gather that the opposition of Sanballat and Tobiah to Nehemiah was not an attack of heathen against the servants of Yahweh, much less was it due to unfriendly feelings towards the Jewish people. It was purely political rivalry, arising probably because Nehemiah's arrival curtailed the authority of Sanballat, and threatened the supremacy of Samaria over Jerusalem.

It is probably not too much to say that Samaria would never have gained the ascendancy over Jerusalem if the Samaritans had been allowed to help in the building of the temple and to join in worship there. Jeroboam of old had seen that the northern district could not remain independent of Judah if the people went on pilgrimage to Jerusalem (I Kings xii. 27). In these later times it was the Judaeans who prevented the Samaritans from coming to worship at Jerusalem, with the result that the Samaritans, though still in their hearts Yahweh-worshippers, were thrown politically into the hands of the heathen. The Samaritans were therefore on terms of better friendship with the surrounding nations, and even with the Persians, than were the Jews;

and this international intercourse naturally brought Samaria to the fore compared with Judah. If only the Jews had wished it, and had followed the teaching of Deutero-Isaiah, Jerusalem could have become a Mecca to which Samaritans, Ammonites, Edomites, Moabites and Arabians would have come in pilgrimage to learn the worship of the one true God.

Now as long as Jerusalem was an undefended town it could be reduced to submission any time by the arrival of the Samaritan army outside its boundaries. Nehemiah therefore made his preparations in secret, and the Samaritans did not learn his plan until he was in a position to begin the work. The Samaritans thought that the work could be stopped in the same way as on the last occasion, and consequently derided the Jews, as well as threatening them with the accusation of rebellion against king Artaxerxes (ii. 19). They soon found however that they had met their match in Nehemiah. Neh. iii. 33–35 (E.V. iv. 1–3) gives another account of the mockery with which they thought to frighten the Jews from the work. When they found however that the work was really going ahead they determined to stop it by force (iv. 2, E.V. iv. 8). The Jews heard of this and set watchmen day and night. The great thing was to get the work done quickly so as to be a defence against such an attack. But an unforeseen difficulty arose: the Jews who were doing the actual building found that the labourers, probably their slaves, were in such poor physical condition that they could not remove the débris and carry the stones as quickly as their masters could build, so that the latter were obliged to stand idle (iv. 4, E.V. iv. 10). We are

not told how the difficulty was overcome, but we may
guess that, rather than risk complete failure by going
so slowly, the upper-class Jews condescended to help
in the labouring work of carrying the burdens—except
the 'gentlemen' of Tekoa, who forgot that they were
the slaves of Yahweh, and thought it beneath their
dignity to do servile work, as it says: "and next unto
them the Tekoites repaired, but their nobles put not
their neck to the work of their Lord" (iii. 5)[1]. The remainder of chapter iv. is in a very bad state of preservation, so that we can only gather the general sense of
what happened. It seems that the Samaritans plotted
a surprise attack on the workers, and that the plot was
discovered by Jews who were living in villages outside
the city and coming in daily to the work. The plan
may have been to get quietly into Jerusalem and attack
the wall-builders from behind, instead of attempting a
frontal attack on the walls. This is suggested by iv. 5
(E.V. iv. 11) "they will not know nor see till we come
into their midst and slay them," and it may explain
the expression מֵאַחֲרֵי לַחוֹמָה "from behind the wall"
(iv. 7) which most probably refers to the place from which
the attack was expected. Being intended as a surprise
attack the plot fell through as soon as it was known, and
Nehemiah was able to recall his men to the walls (iv.
9). This further supports the suggestion that a surprise
attack had been intended in the rear of the workers, so
that instead of keeping them on the walls Nehemiah
had been obliged to hold them in readiness in the open

[1] Perhaps the author of this sneer judged the Tekoites too harshly,
for they were able to undertake a second section of the wall (iii. 27).

places of the city (בצחחיים iv. 7) where the attackers
had been expected to assemble. Now that the chance
of an attack in the rear was much smaller they were
able to return to the walls, and having weapons in
readiness, either girded on or by their side, they were
prepared for any frontal attack. As a further security
against possible surprise attacks by night from inside
the city, all the workmen slept inside the city instead
of returning each evening to their villages. As history
has shown, Jerusalem was a very difficult city to take
by storm if it was defended by a handful of brave men,
and therefore Sanballat, seeing now that the walls were
too far advanced for a frontal attack to have any chance
of success, and seeing that Nehemiah had taken such
precautions against surprise attacks, gave up all hope
of stopping the work by force, and attempted to get
hold of Nehemiah by guile. This is related in chapter vi.
Sanballat and Geshem sent letters suggesting a conference in a village in the plain of Ono, from which
Nehemiah excused himself on the ground of the urgency
of his work. Repeated letters of this sort were sent, and
the last of these said it was commonly reported that
Nehemiah was about to proclaim himself king, and
Sanballat suggested a conference with him lest the matter
should reach the ears of Artaxerxes. Nehemiah bluntly
denied the charge, and accused Sanballat of having invented the story. Meanwhile a vigorous correspondence
was going on between Tobiah and his many confederates
in Judah. These confederates tried to persuade Nehemiah of Tobiah's good intentions, and Tobiah wrote
letters to Nehemiah in the guise of friendly warnings
(vi. 17–19). Tobiah and Sanballat even went so far as

to hire a prophet named Shemaiah to tell Nehemiah that
his life was threatened that night, and to suggest that he
should take refuge in the Holy of Holies of the temple
(vi. 10–13). By his determination and strength of
character Nehemiah was proof against all these wiles,
and the wall was finished. If the date given in our record is reliable the wall was finished in fifty-two days[1],
less than six months from the day when Nehemiah got
the king's permission to undertake the journey. The
story that he has left us, although in parts in such a
poor state of preservation, is sufficient to show how
many and varied were the obstacles in the way of the
work, and how splendidly he overcame them. The
result was much more than the mere restoration of
the city. He secured for Judah and Jerusalem inde-
pendence from Samaria, and gained for Judah a new
reputation in the eyes of the other nations. Hitherto
they had looked up to Samaria, but now they despised
it: the expression in vi. 16 וַיִּפְּלוּ מְאֹד בְּעֵינֵיהֶם "they
fell greatly in their eyes" can scarcely mean anything
else than that the Samaritans fell greatly in the eyes
of the heathen. From this time onwards the power of
Samaria began to wane and that of Judah to increase.

---

[1] Josephus, *Ant.* XI. v. 8, says 2 years 4 months, which equals
852 days, but the shorter period seems more likely from the great haste
with which the work was done. The longer period was presumably
understood (1) by the editor who placed Nehemiah's social reforms,
chapter v., in the middle of the story of the wall-building, and (2) by
the person who placed the words "neither bought I (we) a field," v. 16,
between the two sentences "And I also supported the work of this
wall," and "and all my servants were gathered together unto the work."
The statement that he did not acquire a field is unaccountable in this
connexion unless the writer thought the wall-building occupied a somewhat long period.

Some insight into the social conditions of Nehemiah's
time is given by his account of his reforms in chapter
v. A complaint was made by the people "against their
brethren the Jews." It is quite clear that the com-
plainants were themselves Jews, not only by the use
of the word "brethren" (v. 1) for their oppressors, but
also by the expression "our brethren the Jews" used
by Nehemiah in v. 8 with reference to the same poor
oppressed people. Their complaints were that they
were giving their children as security in order to obtain
food[1], they mortgaged their fields, vineyards and houses,
in order to obtain food in time of famine, they had
borrowed money to pay the king's taxes, they were
selling their children as slaves, and (for this is apparently the only meaning) some of their daughters
had been taken by force. The people responsible for
all this oppression are described as "their brethren the
Jews" and also as "nobles and rulers." The latter terms
are found several times in Nehemiah, and indicate the
people of wealth and position. Nehemiah found them
in power when he first came to Jerusalem, and they
supported him in the building of the walls. They probably were the larger landowners; but their fault consisted in taking advantage of the poverty of their
neighbours and "laying field to field till there was no
room"—a complaint as old as Isaiah. Nehemiah was
able to show that he was really acting in the interests
of the Jews, for he had been buying back Jews from
slavery among the nations, and now he found to his
disgust that it was Jewish nobles who were enslaving

---

[1] Read עֹרְבִים "giving as security" in v. 2 instead of רַבִּים "many."

their poorer brethren and selling them to the heathen. This shameful dealing had only to be exposed to be brought to an end. And so complete was the evidence against them, that they did all that Nehemiah told them, and promised on oath to restore the property they had acquired from their brethren, and to forgo the interest on the money they had lent them.

Nehemiah saw that the restoration of the nation necessitated gathering together as many as possible of the scattered Jews so that they might realize their citizenship and not become fused with other nations. To this end he kept open house in Jerusalem for Jews returning from among the heathen. This is mentioned in v. 17, where the Hebrew text says that he had at his table 150 Jews and rulers, and also the Jews returning from among the heathen. The verse refers probably in the main to the period during which the walls were being built. It was then necessary to provide hospitality for a number of the rulers who were in charge of different parts of the work, and also for those Jews who came out of the country parts and had no homes in Jerusalem. The Greek translators misunderstood the verse, thinking it referred merely to Nehemiah's beneficence to the poor, and therefore omitted the word 'rulers.' vii. 4, speaking of the time when the city walls and gates were finished, says that no houses were built. This does not mean that no houses were standing, but that none of the work of repair had been taken in hand. When however it was necessary for wall-building and for defence to increase the population of the city there was urgent need for more housing accommodation; and in the meanwhile, till

houses were repaired or built, Nehemiah provided food
for the new-comers. When the walls and gates were
completed it was desirable to bring many more inhabitants into Jerusalem, and Nehemiah called a council
of the nobles, rulers, and people to consider the matter
(vii. 5)[1]. Chapter xi. 1 continues the narrative by saying
that the chiefs went and dwelt[2] in Jerusalem, and that
the rest of the people cast lots so that one in ten should
go and dwell in Jerusalem. Others besides (xi. 2)
voluntarily offered to dwell in the city. It is to be noted
that Nehemiah thus made a name for himself, not only
as a wall-builder, but as a restorer of homes: "Also of
Nehemiah the memorial is great; who raised up for us
the walls that were fallen, and set up the gates and bars,
and raised up our homes again," Ben Sira xlix. 13.

Nehemiah's first administration lasted twelve years,
till the thirty-second year of Artaxerxes (Neh. v. 14,
xiii. 6), when he returned to the royal court. It is probable that he returned simply because the period was
ended for which he had permission of absence. This
is a possible translation of xiii. 6: "for in the thirty-
second year of Artaxerxes king of Babylon I came
unto the king, even at the end of the days which I had
requested of the king." This, side by side (as a doub-
let) with another rendering, is found in Lucian's Greek
text εἰς τὸ καιρὸν τῶν ἡμερῶν ὧν ᾐτησάμην παρὰ τοῦ
βασιλέως, καὶ μετὰ τὸ τέλος τῶν ἡμερῶν ὧν ᾐτησάμην

---

[1] This is what the Greek says—εἰς συνοδίας. The Hebrew has been
altered into "that they might be reckoned by genealogy" so as to fit in
with the genealogical list which the Chronicler inserted here.

[2] This is the meaning of the waw consecutive וַיֵּשְׁבוּ. It does not
mean that they were already dwelling in the city (as Batten takes it),
which would be expressed by the participle.

παρὰ τοῦ βασιλέως. Twelve years is perhaps rather long for permission of absence, but the period granted in the first instance may have been extended. In any case we are not told how long it was before he returned to Jerusalem to carry out the policy mentioned in chapter xiii.

As soon as he returned he discovered that Eliashib, the aged high-priest, had given a large chamber in the temple precincts to Tobiah the Ammonite (xiii. 7–9). This was specially galling because Tobiah was not only an Ammonite, but also an enemy of Nehemiah, and this particular room had formerly been used as a store-room for tithes and other temple offerings. The Chronicler in inserting this narrative quotes from Deut. xxiii. 4–6 (E.V. 3–5) the prohibition against Moabites and Ammonites ever entering the congregation, and says that they put the law into practice by separating from Israel all the mixed multitude, i.e. excommunicating foreigners from participating in the temple services (Neh. xiii. 1–3). It would not be surprising if Nehemiah adopted some such policy as this, for it would only be an extension of the policy of a century earlier in excommunicating the Samaritans, but it is perhaps doubtful whether he was able to carry the policy through so completely as is indicated by xiii. 3 "they separated from Israel all the mixed multitude," and xiii. 30 "then cleansed I them from all strangers."

The next evil that he found needing correction was that the dues to the Levites had been withheld (xiii. 10–13). Consequently many of the Levites had left the city and gone to earn their living on the land, and

the temple services were neglected. This may also
account for the room being vacant which was given to
Tobiah, since the tithes and offerings had ceased. All
this can readily be understood when we remember that
Eliashib the high-priest was an aged man as is shown
by his having a grandson of marriageable age (xiii. 28).
Nehemiah gathered together the scattered Levites to
Jerusalem, rebuked the rulers for allowing these abuses,
and appointed treasurers to look after and distribute
the tithes.

Then he observed that the sabbath was being broken
(xiii. 15–21). Not only were country people treading
out their grapes in the winepress on the holy day, but
they laded their asses with the fruits of harvest and
brought them to Jerusalem and sold them on the sabbath. More objectionable still was it to see Jews being
corrupted by foreigners, for Tyrian merchants came
with fish and other wares and sold them to Jews in the
city on the sabbath. Again Nehemiah rebuked the
rulers for allowing this to go on. He himself took
strong measures in the case of those who trafficked on
the sabbath, though there is no record of his interfering
with the people who trod the winepresses. He ordered
that the gates should be kept shut all the sabbath; and
when he found that the traders stopped outside the gates
(to do business outside Jerusalem, as the Greek version
of xiii. 20 tells us, Jewish citizens being presumably
permitted to pass through the gates) he threatened
them with violence, and they came no more on the
sabbath. In trying to enforce the fourth commandment
Nehemiah was following in the steps of earlier religious
leaders. Amos (viii. 5) rebuked the people for longing

for the end of the new moon and sabbath festivals so
that they could go on with their business; Jeremiah
especially complained of their carrying burdens and
bringing them into Jerusalem on the sabbath (Jer. xvii.
21–27)[1]; Ezekiel continually complained of the profa-
nation of the sabbath (*e.g.* xx. 13, xxii. 8, xxiii. 38).

The last reform that we are told Nehemiah undertook was directed against mixed marriages (xiii. 23–30).
Here the original memoir has been worked over by
the Chronicler, and not much of Nehemiah's own narrative remains. But we should have been prepared for
such a policy: he had been bringing the scattered Jews
into Jerusalem from living among the heathen, he had
gathered the Levites together into the city, he had
violently cast out the Ammonite who had set up house
in the temple precincts, and it was natural that he
should pursue the policy of putting every barrier between Jew and non-Jew. When he found Jews married
to women of Ashdod, with children who spoke the dialect of Ashdod, he felt that the loss of the national language would result in the loss of the sense of Jewish
nationality. Consequently he took the strongest
measures to prevent a repetition of such unions. Our
present text also mentions unions with women of Ammon and Moab, but that is probably an addition by
the same hand that wrote xiii. 1–3 quoting from Deuteronomy against those two tribes, for the language
that the children spoke is particularly mentioned as
that of Ashdod. The climax came when the aged
Eliashib allowed his grandson to marry a daughter of

---

[1] But the passage has been thought by some critics, including Kuenen,
Cheyne and H. P. Smith, to be post-exilic.

Sanballat (xiii. 28). He was probably one of the younger sons of Joiada, but even so there was always the possibility that his elder brothers might die and he might become high-priest, and in any case it was unthinkable (to Nehemiah) that the high-priest should be so closely related to the arch-enemy of Israel. Nehemiah drove the offender away, probably leaving him to go and find a home with his father-in-law in Samaria. Josephus mistakenly attached to this event the origin of the Samaritan temple on Mount Gerizim, but to that we must return later.

CHAPTER IX

DATA FROM ELEPHANTINE

SEVERAL times already mention has been made of a colony of Jews at Elephantine or Yeb in Upper Egypt. The discovery of various papyri there since the beginning of this century has given us much material for consideration, and the contemporary evidence provided by them has certainly altered some of our earlier ideas. There may be yet further surprises for us. Besides the sumptuous editions of texts with which we have been supplied by Sayce and Cowley and by Sachau, a number of books and articles dealing with them have appeared. The most important of these will be found in the bibliography at the beginning of this book. It is not proposed to add to these discussions, but only to mention those points which affect the history and religious ideas of our period.

Sachau's papyrus 6, commonly called the Passover papyrus, is of great importance to us, as it gives directions for the feast of unleavened cakes; but unfortunately about half of most of the lines is missing, and there is in consequence a difference of opinion as to the source from which the directions were issued. The author and receivers of the letter are clearly stated in a docket, "To my brethren, Jedoniah and his associates the Judaean garrison: your brother Hananiah." The date is clearly given as the fifth year of Darius, *i.e.* 419 B.C. After that comes the sentence on which there is disagreement .מן מלכא שליח על ארש.. followed by a gap of half a line. Sachau and most others have taken it to mean "(a rescript) having been sent from the king to Arsham." Arsham we know as the satrap of Egypt, and if this translation were correct it would mean that Darius the king sent out a royal edict as to how the passover was to be kept at Elephantine, and that the edict was sent through the usual channels, *i.e.* to Arsham the satrap, and by him forwarded to the Jews. We can well believe that a Persian king would authorize a subject race to build their temple, and even that he might pay a grant out of the royal treasury towards such an object, or even remit taxation from the priests, but it is too much to expect anyone to believe that he would concern himself with the minute details of a festival and the restrictions as to food and drinks on that occasion. W. R. Arnold[1] was the first to point out the impossibility of the rendering given above. He proposed that שליח did not refer to a thing but to a person, namely Hananiah the author of the letter, and he translated the passage thus, "This year, the fifth year of Darius the king, being sent from the king to Arsames [I visited the city of Jerusalem]," suggesting for the missing words some such clause as that given in the brackets. This was challenged at once by Elhorst[2] on the grounds that the added words are not sufficiently

---

[1] "Passover Papyrus from Elephantine," *Journal of Biblical Literature*, 1912, p. 4.

[2] *Journal of Biblical Literature*, Sept. 1912, p. 147.

explicit, and that it would really be necessary to add something like "I visited the city of Jerusalem when the priests gave me directions for the celebration of the feast of the passover in order that I might deliver them to you," for which there is not room in the missing half-line. But in fact there is no need to be so prolix. If the sentence had originally run "I came to Jerusalem and I received an order for you from the priests" it would exactly fill the space and would say all that was required. Sprengling[1] objected to Arnold's translation on grounds of syntax, that according to other usage the participle שליח should be preceded by a conjunction 'when,' 'after' or 'because.' But with such scanty examples of the Aramaic of the period one can scarcely say that the construction is impossible, and it is better for the present to follow Arnold's translation than to believe, unless we are compelled by further evidence, that Darius II concerned himself with Jewish ritual. We take it then that these directions came from Jerusalem, and were delivered to the Elephantine community by Hananiah. The nature of the directions for the feast, and their relations with the Jewish codes of law, will be considered later. Just now our interest lies in the author of the letter Hananiah, a common Jewish name. He appears again in Sachau's papyrus 11, where an Elephantine Jew says, "You know the affliction which, for no reason at all, has rested upon us since Hananiah came to Egypt until now." As we have seen that Hananiah probably came to Egypt just before he wrote papyrus 6

[1] "The Aramaic Papyri of Elephantine in English," *American Journal of Theology*, July 1917 and July 1918.

in 419 B.C., this letter was written after then, but before 410 when the temple at Elephantine was destroyed. It is somewhat tempting to follow Sachau's suggestion that this Jew Hananiah, a high Persian official, is the same as Hanani, Nehemiah's brother, whose report at Susa in 445 led to Nehemiah's journey.

By far the most important of these Elephantine discoveries is a letter which appears in duplicate in Sachau's papyri 1 and 2, relating to the destruction of the Jewish temple at Elephantine in the 14th year of Darius, *i.e.* 410 B.C. Arsham the satrap had left Egypt to pay a visit to the royal court at Susa, and in his absence a plot was concocted between the priests of Chnub who dwelt at Yeb and Widarnag the military captain. Widarnag sent a letter to his son who was in command of the fortress at Syene, which was on the river bank opposite the island of Yeb, ordering him to destroy the Jewish temple. This he did very thoroughly, knocking down all the stone structures, burning the woodwork, and plundering everything of value. The Jews not only showed their grief by sackcloth, fasting, and prayer to Yahu, but they seem also to have had their vengeance: the language is not quite clear, but it appears that Widarnag as well as those who perpetrated the outrage met a violent death. In order that the temple might be restored the Jews wrote various letters, (1) to Bagohi, the governor of Judah, (2) to Jehohanan the high-priest, and his companions the priests of Jerusalem, and to Awstan the brother of Anani, and to the freemen (or nobles) of the Jews. These letters were sent at the time of the outrage, and received no reply. In 408–407 B.C. they wrote further letters, viz. (3) to Delaiah and Shelemiah, the sons of Sanballat the governor of Samaria, and (4) to Bagohi, the governor of Judah. Copies of this fourth letter have been preserved, and from them we gain all our information. The letter brings us into a circle of people several of whom we know already. There is Arsham, mentioned in other papyri, but known before the discovery of the papyri as Ἀρξάνης who Ktesias[1] tells us was satrap of Egypt at the beginning of the reign of Darius II. There is Sanballat, whom we knew as the bitter opponent of Nehemiah. Ezr. x. 6 and Neh. xii. 22 had made us acquainted with Jehohanan the high-priest in Ezra's time. And Josephus, whom we only half believed, had told us a sad story about Jehohanan and Bagohi. Josephus' story is as follows[2]: John the high-priest had a brother named Jesus, and Bagoses (or Bagoas) "the general of the army of another Artaxerxes" had promised to secure Jesus the high-priesthood. As a result of this there followed a quarrel between the two brothers in the temple, in which John killed Jesus. Bagoses was very angry and forced his way into the temple, claiming that he was purer than the corpse, and punished the Jews for seven years, laying a tax of fifty drachmae on every lamb sacrificed. Josephus made two blunders in recording this event, which almost justified its rejection until the papyrus showed that there really was a Bagohi contemporary with the high-priest John. One of the blunders was in the amount of the fine—whatever it

---

[1] *Persika*, XVIII. 78, ed. Gilmore, p. 168.
[2] *Ant.* XI. vii. 1.

really was it was something in shekels and not in drachmae at that time[1]. The other blunder was describing Bagoses as a general of another Artaxerxes' army. This was a troublesome error, because there was a well-known military general of Artaxerxes III (Ochus) named Bagoses, and great difficulty was experienced in trying to fit this incident into his career. Our Bagoses, the satrap of Judah in Artaxerxes II's reign should properly have been described as ὕπαρχος; and even if he was given the title of στρατηγός which satraps in Seleucid times bore, he could not have been strategus of an army, for under Persian rule the army was independent of the satrap[2]. However it is easy to see now how Josephus made the mistake, by confusing the sub-satrap of Judah with the famous general. As the papyrus shows that Bagohi was governor of Judah in 410 and 407 B.C. under Darius II, it is easy to suppose that he still held office under Artaxerxes II (Mnemon) who came to the throne in 404, and that the murder took place somewhere in the neighbourhood of 400 B.C. Josephus does not say that John was punished in any way, and rather suggests that he retained his high-priesthood till he died a natural death: "Now when John had departed this life, his son Jaddua succeeded in the high-priesthood[3]." Moreover he was still in office in Ezra's time, which was, as we shall see, probably in Artaxerxes II's reign.

Now let us return to Sanballat. Thirty-seven years had elapsed between his first conflict with Nehemiah

---

[1] Willrich, *Judaica*.

[2] Meyer, art. 'Satrap' in *Encycl. Britannica*, ed. xi.

[3] *Ant.* XI. vii. 2.

and the date of the papyrus. If he was then a middle-aged man such as would hold a responsible position, he would be getting aged in 407 B.C., and this is what is suggested by the fact that though he is described as governor the letter is addressed to his sons. They were evidently acting on his behalf. What was the purpose of the community at Elephantine in writing all these letters? It certainly cannot have been for political authority to rebuild the temple, for the satraps in Judah and Samaria would have no authority in the satrapy of Egypt. Nor is there any suggestion that they were appealing for funds. All they ask for is that letters should be written to them. Probably what they wished for was written evidence from the Palestinian authorities that they were practising the authorized Jewish cult, so that they could lay this evidence before Arsham in seeking his permission to rebuild their temple. Much surprise has been expressed that these Jews should appeal in their difficulty to the sons of Sanballat the enemy of Nehemiah. How, it was asked, could faithful Jews appeal to the enemy of their religion? But as we have already seen, it is quite possible that Sanballat was himself an Israelite, and in any case his antagonism to Nehemiah was purely political. We can imagine the Elephantine Jews thinking that the best recommendation of their cult would come from the high-priest at Jerusalem, and from the Persian governor of Judah; but if they failed, a recommendation from the governor of the other Israelite province, namely Samaria, would do just as well. At any rate they tried the high-priest and the governor of Judah

first, and when they got no reply they wrote again
to the governor of Judah and also to the sons
of the governor of Samaria. To this they did get a
reply, but in two respects not such a reply as they
wished. First it was verbal and not written, which
would not be much use as evidence to Arsham; and
secondly it did not authorize burnt offerings. They
had specially stated in their letter that they wished
not only to rebuild their temple, but to offer meal
offerings, incense, and burnt offerings, as had been
done before. Sachau's papyrus 3 is a memorandum
of a verbal message which the bearer had received
from Bagohi and Delaiah: "Memorandum of what
Bagohi and Delaiah said to me. Memorandum as
follows: You may speak in Egypt to Arsham with
regard to the altar-house of the God of Heaven, which
was built formerly, before Cambyses, in the fortress
Yeb, which that accursed Widarnag destroyed in the
14th year of Darius, so that it may be rebuilt in its
place as it was before, and that meal offerings and
incense may be offered on that altar in accordance
with former practice." The omission of the burnt
offering is probably intentional. The Jews at Elephantine could no doubt easily justify their practice
of offering sacrifices elsewhere than at Jerusalem, in
spite of all that was said in Deuteronomy, by the
fact that they were outside Palestine. The Jews in
Jerusalem may have felt rather uncertain about the
point, and may have wished rather to shut their eyes
to what was going on, or to accept a compromise.
This uncertainty probably accounted for their not
replying in the first instance, and for their omitting

the burnt offerings when they did reply. In the same way the Passover papyrus of twelve years previously had given no directions for the slaying of the lambs (the passover proper) but only for the feast of unleavened cakes. It is worth noticing that the governors of Judah and Samaria sent a joint reply. In their eyes at any rate there was no difference between the religions of the two provinces. The distinction between animal sacrifices, and the offerings of incense and meal, is also referred to in Sachau's papyrus 5. The papyrus is so mutilated that one cannot make it out with any certainty, but it looks as if the writers, five Jewish notables from Elephantine, were offering a large bribe to someone whom they addressed as "our lord" if the temple was rebuilt and incense and meal offerings were made there, even if no animal sacrifices were allowed. It is doubtful whether the Jews ever rebuilt their temple at Elephantine, for almost directly after this Egypt threw off the Persian yoke, and the Jews would therefore lose their protectors. The Strasbourg papyrus[1] tends to support this, because the Jews asserted that they had remained loyal to the Persians when the other inhabitants of Egypt revolted. It seems as if when Arsham returned to Egypt he found what had happened, and how the Jews had had revenge on Widarnag and his men. The Jews felt obliged to justify themselves, and therefore they wrote this letter, apparently to Arsham, in which they say that they had remained loyal when the Egyptians revolted, and they relate how Widarnag

[1] Edited by Euting: *Mémoires presentées par divers savants à l'Académie des Inscriptions*, 1e série, tom. xi., 2e partie, p. 297.

had damaged the fortress of Yeb, especially by filling up the well, but they carefully say nothing about the wrongs that they themselves and their temple had suffered.

The papyri have information to give us about the religion of the Jews of Elephantine, and such information as to raise serious doubts as to the purity of their monotheism. The most startling fact is to be found in Sachau's papyrus 18, which is a list of people who subscribed or were taxed two shekels apiece for Yahweh. The heading of the MS. is "On the 3rd of Phamenot of the 5th year of...[probably the fifth year of Darius II, *i.e.* 6th June 419]. These are the names of the Jewish army, who gave money for the God Yahu, man for man, 2 shekels of silver." After the list of names the total is given as follows: "The silver which was found on this day in the hand of Jedoniah bar Gemariah, in the month Phamenot—

> Silver 31 karshin 8 shekels
> to wit: for Yahu 12 karshin 6 shekels
> for Ashim-Bethel 7 karshin
> for Anath-Bethel 12 karshin "[1].

It is really rather distressing to find that of the money ostensibly subscribed for Yahweh nearly two-thirds is appropriated for two other deities. It is evident that in some way these other deities are connected with Yahweh as the inscription at the heading says that all the money is for Yahweh. Van Hoonacker points to the discrepancy between the total as given here, 31 karshin 8 shekels, and the actual total obtained by

---

[1] 1 karsh = 10 shekels.

adding all the sums of 2 shekels, which is 24 or 26 karshin, and he thinks in consequence that the 31 karshin 8 shekels is an independent subscription and not a total of the foregoing sums. Moreover it is followed by a few more subscriptions of 2 shekels. A more probable explanation of the discrepancy is that Jedoniah had some money in hand before the levy of 2 shekels a head was made.

The chief point we must enquire into about the deities here mentioned is whether they were of Canaanite origin and imported into Egypt when the Jews immigrated, or whether they were Egyptian deities whom the Jews learnt to worship after their arrival in the country. It is clear in the first place that we are dealing with Semitic and not with Egyptian deities. The names of Ashim (אשם), Anath (ענת), and Bethel (ביתאל) appear independently as deities. Bethel occurs as the name of a Phoenician god. Several proper names are found in our papyri compounded with Bethel, viz. Bethel-nathan (Sachau's papyrus 34), Bethel-aqab (pap. 17), Bethel-itaqim (pap. 25), and Ḥaram-bethel is the name of a god. There may be traces of the name in the Old Testament, but it is difficult to prove this because we cannot be sure whether the god or the town of Bethel is intended. Jer. xlviii. 13 is such a case: "Moab shall be ashamed of Chemosh, as the house of Israel was ashamed of Bethel their confidence." Anath was an old Semitic deity, whose name is preserved in the Old Testament in Beth-anath, Anath, and Anathoth. A man named Anathi is mentioned in papyrus 18, and, what is most extraordinary, a deity named Anath-Yahu in papyrus

32. Ashim (the vocalization of which is uncertain) is not well known, but is probably connected with Ashima (אֲשִׁימָא) a deity mentioned in II Kings xvii. 30, and probably to be read in Amos viii. 14, "They that swear by Ashima of Samaria (אַשְׁמַת שֹׁמְרוֹן, generally taken as 'the sin of Samaria'), and say 'As thy God liveth, O Dan,' and 'As thy Dod (reading דֹּדְךָ instead of M.T. דֶּרֶךְ) liveth, O Beersheba,'" Dod, or Dodo, being a deity worshipped by the children of Gad and mentioned on the Moabite Stone, line 12. Now II Kings xvii. 31 not only mentions Ashima as one of the deities worshipped by the Samaritans, but also Anammelek, which is an assimilation of Anath-melek. This is not by any means to be taken as evidence that the worship of these deities was introduced by immigrants from Hamath and Sepharvaim. But it is evidence that Ashima and Anath-melek were worshipped at Samaria in the time when II Kings was compiled, or at least that it was still remembered in those days that they had been worshipped there. That they were worshipped at Samaria suggests at once association of these deities with Yahweh, and this is further borne out by the name of a Goddess Anath-Yahu in papyrus 32. On the analogy of Ashtar-Chemosh on the Moabite Stone (line 17), meaning Ashtar the consort of Chemosh, this would mean Anath the consort of Yahu. As the name Anath-Bethel also occurs it is possible that Bethel was identified with Yahweh—not a surprising identification for anyone who knew the story of Jacob and his mazzebah which he called Bethel, Gen. xxviii. 19–22. In that case both Anath and

Ashim would probably be consorts of Yahweh. It is worth mentioning that in papyrus 32 an oath is taken by Masgida and by Anath-Yahu. The former is not properly a deity, but a place of worship (either sanctuary, or mazzebah, or altar, cf. the Arabic 'masgid,' 'a place of worship'), and reminds us that such an oath was permitted by the Pharisees in our Lord's time, "whosoever shall swear by the sanctuary it is nothing," Matth. xxiii. 16. Somewhat similar is the origin of the deity Haram-Bethel, for haram is of course properly speaking the sacred enclosure or holy ground of a sanctuary. Now it has been suggested that the intercommunication between Elephantine and Jerusalem was such that the religious ideas in the one were likely to be the same as in the other, that in all probability other gods were associated with Yahweh-worship at Jerusalem as late as 400 B.C., and that traces of such polytheism have simply been removed from the Bible by later editors. In support of this such passages are quoted as Is. lxv. where heathen and idolatrous worship is condemned. But that passage has already been seen to refer to half-Jews who followed their heathen parents rather than their Jewish parents. A more instructive passage is Jer. xliv. In that chapter Jeremiah utters a prophecy against the Jews of Egypt and especially those "in the country of Pathros," *i.e.* Upper Egypt, which the Greeks called the Thebaid, stretching from Memphis to Syene. He represents these Jews as saying that they will continue to offer incense and pour out drink offerings to the Queen of Heaven as they and their forefathers had done in Judah and Jerusalem (xliv. 16, 17), but they go on to attribute their misfortunes to the fact that they had left off offering incense to her. This seems to be strong contemporary evidence that the worship of the Queen of Heaven was a Jewish cult, practised in Judah and even in Jerusalem, but that it had been falling into desuetude in the period just before the capture of the city by Nebuchadrezzar. Jeremiah was evidently astonished, not merely at the existence of the cult among the Thebaid Jews, but at its recrudescence. It looks as if the misfortunes of Judah just before the fall of Jerusalem led many people to seek help from other kinds of worship, including some that had been practised formerly but had almost died out. Ezek. viii. 10–17 shows how some of the people were led to seek help in foreign cults—Tammuz, the Sun, and unclean vermin. Now it is quite likely that our colony at Elephantine dates from the time of Jeremiah. For Pseudo-Aristeas, § 13, says, that Jews came to Egypt in the time of the Persian (presumably Cambyses, the first to enter Egypt), and also, earlier, Jews were sent to Egypt to fight for Psammetichus against the Ethiopians[1]. Aristeas is utterly unreliable in many things, especially with regard to the LXX, but he may quite well represent a true tradition as to the origin of the Jewish military colony at Elephantine. They must have been earlier than Cambyses, for their temple was built before his time (Sachau's papyrus I, lines 13, 14). We know from Herodotus II. 159–161, that Psammetichus II, who reigned 594–589 B.C., fought against the Ethiopians, and the fact that

[1] See Sachau, *Aramäische Papyrus u. Ostraka*, 1911, vol. I. pp. xiv and 37.

Judah was hastening to its fall at that time, and that many Jews were leaving the country, would give a simple explanation of the origin of the military colony at Elephantine. It would be then these very people whose defection from Yahweh caused such grief and anger to Jeremiah. In the letter of their descendants of 407 B.C. Yahweh is repeatedly called the God of Heaven, and as we have seen that Anath-Yahu was in all probability a consort of Yahweh she may well have been called by the title that Jeremiah uses—the Queen of Heaven. The importance of this conclusion is very great, for it means that the polytheism which we find at the end of the fifth century at Elephantine was a relic of Judaean polytheism that had been revived by the experiences of the immigrants at a time when it was dying out in Palestine. There is however evidence that even in Elephantine the polytheism was passing away by the end of the fifth century. Only a mere handful of proper names are compounded with the names of these other deities, while a very large number are compounded with Yahu. The temple is always spoken of as the temple of Yahu, and there is no record of incense or any other offering being made to the other deities. It may well be that the affliction spoken of in papyrus 11, which had come on the Jewish community since Hananiah's arrival in Egypt, was due to an attempt on his part to root out the remains of heathen practices, or perhaps to an attempt to enforce an obedience to the Deuteronomic law of the One Sanctuary[1].

[1] W. R. Arnold, *loc. cit.*, p. 30.

CHAPTER X

EZRA AND THE LAW

A GREAT deal of interest hangs round the name of Ezra. The Chronicler made him his chief hero. In various early Jewish and Christian circles it was thought that he had re-written from inspired memory the whole Old Testament which had been destroyed[1]. Mohammed falsely accused the Jews of calling Ezra Son of God[2]. Strange miraculous stories about him grew up among Mohammedan commentators[3]. The Higher Critics made him the author of the Priestly Code or the compiler of the Pentateuch. And some of the latest critics go to the opposite extreme and deny his existence altogether. It is one of the curiosities of modern criticism that the most violent attack on the existence of Ezra comes from Prof. Torrey, who, by restoring the original order of the narrative, has done more than anyone else to make Ezra live before our eyes.

The question of Ezra's existence must be left for the moment until we have collected and considered all that is told of him. We shall then be in a position to decide whether the assumption that he was a real person has enriched or contradicted the history of the period.

[1] IV Esdras (English II Esdras) xiv. 20–48, Iren. III. xxiv. 1, Clem. Alex. *Strom.* I. 22. 149, Tert. *De Cult. Fem.* I. 3.

[2] *Koran*, Sura 9.

[3] See d'Herbelot, *Bibliothèque Orientale*, s.v. 'Ozair.'

To anyone reading the English Bible it appears that
both Ezra and Nehemiah were at work at Jerusalem
at the same time in the reign of Artaxerxes, and
occasionally both of them are on the scene simultane-
ously. It is even probable that in the form in which
the book originally left the hands of the Chronicler
the same impression was given and intended. And
yet the description of the work they did gives the lie
to this. Even though here and there we find their
names occurring together, each of them appears as the
sole leader. True, their offices were different: one was
a Persian satrap, and the other a priest and scribe.
And to a great extent their work was different. But
their work did overlap a little, and it is difficult to
believe that both, at about the same time, could have
taken independent action in the matter of mixed
marriages without any reference to one another. It is
said of both of them that they came to Jerusalem in
the reign of Artaxerxes, but without specifying which
is intended of the three kings of that name. It may
well be that the sources the Chronicler used intended
two different kings, but that the Chronicler supposed
they were one and the same. It was therefore quite
natural for the Chronicler to add Nehemiah's name
by the side of Ezra's at the reading of the law in
Neh. viii. 9, for on such an important occasion Nehemiah must have been there if he was living in
Jerusalem. That the verse has been interfered with
is shown by the uncertainty of the text: the Hebrew
has "Nehemiah, who was the Tirshatha, and Ezra the
the priest the scribe," the Greek of I Esdr. ix. 49 has
"And Attarate (*i.e.* Tirshatha) said to Ezra the high

priest and reader," and the later Greek version of
Neh. viii. 9 has "And Nehemiah said, and Ezra the
priest and scribe." In the same way Nehemiah's name
has been added to the list of those who signed the
covenant in Neh. x. 2 (E.V. 1), but there again the
text is uncertain for the Greek uncials agree against
the Hebrew and the Lucianic Greek text in omitting
the title 'Tirshatha.' Similarly Ezra's name has crept
into the account of the dedication of the walls
(Neh. xii. 36), and Nehemiah's name into the Greek
text of I Esdr. v. 40 (cf. the parallel Hebrew text,
Ezr. ii. 63). All these are such evident insertions that
we may say that the sources the Chronicler used did
not suggest that Ezra and Nehemiah were contemporary at Jerusalem.

Now when Ezra was working in Jerusalem the city
was fairly thickly populated, as witness the crowd that
collected when he made his prayer and confession
(Ezr. x. 1). These were all from Jerusalem, as contrasted with those who came from the surrounding
country within three days (Ezr. x. 9). This had not
been the case in Nehemiah's time, and he had had to
take special measures to increase the population of
the city (Neh. vii. 4). When Ezra was giving thanks
he said that God had extended His mercy to them
"to give us a reviving, to set up the house of our God,
to repair the ruins thereof, and to give us a wall (גָּדֵר)
in Judah and Jerusalem." This is not, it is true, the
usual word for a city wall, though it can be so used
(cf. Mic. vii. 11), and it is a little strange that Judah
as well as Jerusalem is mentioned; but it is difficult
to take it purely figuratively after the concrete refer-

ence to the temple and its ruins. But of course
Nehemiah's wall was a protection, not only to Jerusalem, but also to all Judah. Whereas, if the expression
is to be taken figuratively and dated before Nehemiah,
it is difficult to see what it could be figurative of, or
what was the reviving that had been granted in those
dark days.

Comparing the lists of high-priests in Neh. xii. 11,
and xii. 22, we see that Jonathan was the same as
Johanan, and was the grandson of Eliashib. Now
Ezra was contemporary with Jehohanan, who is described in Ezr. x. 6 as Eliashib's son, a term often
loosely used for grandson (cf. Gen. xxix. 5, xxxi. 28,
43, Ruth iv. 17); and Nehemiah was contemporary
with Eliashib (Neh. iii. 1). Thus Ezra would be ap-
proximately two generations later than Nehemiah.
And it is striking to find that in the chronological list
in Neh. xii. 26 the period over which the names of the
porters has been given is described by the names of
the three most important people in successive generations: "These were in the days of Joiakim, the son of
Jeshua, the son of Josadak, and in the days of Nehemiah the governor, and of Ezra the priest the scribe."

Lastly we have a piece of contemporary evidence
from Sachau's papyri 1 and 2 (see page 164), which
show that Jehohanan was high-priest in Jerusalem
about 408 B.C. This makes it quite clear that Ezra
belongs to the reign of Artaxerxes II, which began
in 404 B.C., and Nehemiah to the reign of Artaxerxes I
(464-424 B.C.). The year of Nehemiah's journey is
given in his Memoirs, Neh. ii. 1, as the twentieth of
Artaxerxes, and that will therefore be 444 B.C. The

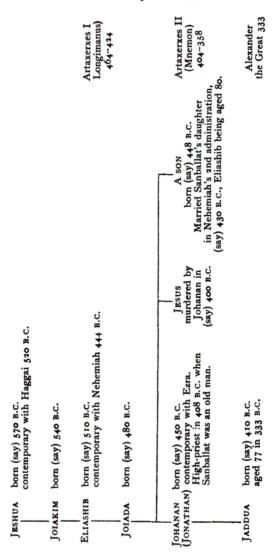

Artaxerxes I
Longimanus
464–424

Artaxerxes II
(Mnemon)
404–358

Alexander
the Great 333

JESHUA   born (say) 570 B.C.
          contemporary with Haggai 520 B.C.

JOIAKIM   born (say) 540 B.C.

ELIASHIB born (say) 510 B.C.
          contemporary with Nehemiah 444 B.C.

JOIADA   born (say) 480 B.C.

JESUS
murdered by
Johanan in
(say) 400 B.C.

A SON
born (say) 448 B.C.
Married Sanballat's daughter
in Nehemiah's 2nd administration,
(say) 430 B.C., Eliashib being aged 80.

JOHANAN   born (say) 450 B.C.
(JONATHAN) contemporary with Ezra.
          High-priest in 408 B.C. when
          Sanballat was an old man.

JADDUA   born (say) 410 B.C.
          aged 77 in 333 B.C.

date given for Ezra's journey is not so certain, for the "seventh year" of Ezra vii. 7 is due to the Chronicler, and there is no year mentioned in Ezra's own Memoirs. The table given opposite shows that it is possible to construct a genealogical tree of the high-priests whose names we know, which is perfectly consistent with all the data. The years of the birth of the high-priests are of course merely conjectural.

The original order of the story of Ezra as it left the hands of the Chronicler was Ezr. vii., viii., Neh. vii. 70–viii. 18[1], Ezr. ix., x., Neh. ix., x. (see page 30). It begins in Ezr. vii. 1–5, with a genealogy of Ezra by the Chronicler. He gives parts of this genealogy in several places, viz. here, and in the parallel passage in I Esdr. viii. 1 f. (where codex B omits three of the names and has two or three different); Neh. xi. 11 and I Chron. ix. 11 (which insert Meraioth between Zadok and Ahitub); I Chron. v. 29 ff. (E.V. vi. 3 ff.) which has six extra names; and I Chron. vi. 35 ff. (E.V. vi. 50 ff.), agreeing as far as it goes with I Chron. v. 29 ff. But the chief point to notice is that according to II Kings xxv. 18 Seraiah went into captivity under Nebuchadnezzar, and according to I Chron. v. 41 (E.V. vi. 15) this was the fate of his son Jehozadak. In making Ezra the son of this Seraiah, the Chronicler is deliberately cutting out the whole period of the Exile, as he did in his history II Chron. xxxvi. 20, and even if there is any foundation for the genealogy it probably only means that Ezra claimed to be descended from Seraiah some six generations earlier. The longer list as given in I Chron. v. 29 ff. would then be quite possible

---

[1] For the verse numeration see note on page 31.

as far as the number of names is concerned, for counting three and a half generations to a century the twenty-two generations would just stretch from Merenptah (1215 B.C.) to the Exile (587 B.C.).

Ezr. vii. 1–10 is the Chronicler's introduction to the Ezra story, and the mention of his arrival in Jerusalem (vii. 8) anticipates what comes later, for in chapter viii. there is a long first-person account of how the caravan set out. This is sufficient to show that the narrative beginning in Ezr. viii. 15 is not by the Chronicler, and is an earlier source, possibly even from the pen of Ezra himself. But before we come to this we find a section in Aramaic, Ezr. vii. 12–26. Like the Aramaic sections that we have already dealt with it has been excerpted by the Chronicler from an earlier work; like the other Aramaic sections it purports to give a royal decree, and like them also it has covered a small residuum of fact with masses of exaggeration intended to glorify Israel. The amplification may have been done by the Chronicler, or by the editor of the Aramaic book. If it was the latter we must assume that he was a man like-minded with the Chronicler. This is probable enough; and indeed, since the Chronicler is very much of one mind with Ezra, we may go further, and suggest that Ezra founded a school of thought in which the Aramaic writer grew up, and of which the Chronicler himself was a later disciple. This is more likely than the supposition that the Chronicler was the first and only writer who set himself to revise history along these lines. The historical residuum of the decree when the exaggerations have been removed would be that Ezra was sent by the king Artaxerxes to Jerusalem with a caravan of Jews, that he had the king's permission to enforce the Jewish law on all the Jews of the province, to collect free-will offerings in Babylonia, to convey them to Jerusalem, and to see that they were duly expended for the service of the temple. The rest of the decree, with its recognition by Artaxerxes of the God of Heaven as worshipped at Jerusalem, the enormous gifts to the temple made by the king, the far-reaching powers conferred upon Ezra, may be neglected as far as history is concerned; but it is of interest as showing a phase of Jewish thought of a century or so later. Of interest for the same reason are the two verses, Ezr. vii. 27, 28, which immediately follow the decree. Whether these are really Ezra's words which have lost their introduction, or whether the Chronicler wrote them, it is interesting to notice in them the process of materializing the Jewish religion. Deutero-Isaiah had spoken of Yahweh being beautified (Is. xliv. 23, xlix. 3), or Israel being beautified (lv. 5), meaning in the first case the renown gained by Yahweh for keeping His pledged word, and in the second the moral perfecting of Israel. Trito-Isaiah nearly a century later also speaks of Yahweh (lx. 21, lxi. 3) and Israel (lx. 9) being beautified; but side by side with this he uses the word in the sense of beautifying the temple by establishing the system of sacrifices (Is. lx. 7), or by improving its material structure (lx. 13). It is in the former sense of beautifying the temple by establishing the sacrificial ritual that the word is used here in Ezr. vii. 27.

Ezra's real narrative begins at Ezr. viii. 15. He gath-

ered the members of the caravan together at the river
Ahavah, and there they rested three days. During
that time, according to the Hebrew text, he searched
among the people and the priests and found no Levites.
This is evidently wrong, as even in P all priests are
Levites, although all Levites are not priests. I Esdr.
viii. 41 f. tries to correct it saying "And I considered
them; and having found none of the priests and of
the Levites I sent...." In view of the fact that the
sequel only mentions Levites and Nethinim as being
fetched it is probable that the word 'priests' is an
addition, and that the text originally read "And I
viewed the people and found there none of the sons
of Levi." The emendation of Ezr. viii. 17 has already
been referred to[1], from which it appears that chosen
men were sent by Ezra with a message to his brother
Iddo, the chief priest of a sanctuary at a town called
Casiphia. They were successful in their quest, and
brought back some 40 Levites and 220 Nethinim.
Then Ezra proclaimed a fast to intreat God's protection on the journey. He would have liked to have
asked for an escort, but was ashamed to do so after
what he had said about the protecting hand of God—
a little touch which is much too life-like to have been
invented by the Chronicler. The sort of thing the
Chronicler could produce was very different, and is
seen only a few verses further on (viii. 26, 27) in the
fabulous wealth which they took to Jerusalem. The
prayers of Ezra and the company were heard, and
they reached Jerusalem and safely deposited the
treasures in the hands of the treasurers—two priests

[1] P. 53.

and two Levites (Ezr. viii. 33), as had previously been appointed by Nehemiah (Neh. xiii. 13). Sacrifices were offered—again exaggerated by the Chronicler—and the decrees were delivered to the satraps. Our text says "the satraps and the governors beyond the River"; the two terms are synonymous, and one of the two must be an explanatory addition. The satraps "supported the people and the house of God" (Ezr. viii. 36), which means apparently that they gave assistance in money or kind, for Neh. vii. 70 which continues the narrative speaks of the contributions given by the heads of families, by the Tirshatha (*i.e.* the governor or satrap of Judah), and by the people. Then the whole company went and dwelt in their various cities, so that by the seventh month all the children of Israel, *i.e.* those who had returned with this latest detachment, were in their cities. On the first day of that seventh month the people gathered together (Neh. viii. 1) and requested Ezra to read the Law to them. This he did.

It has so often been stated that Ezra's Law Book which he read to the people was the priestly code or the whole Pentateuch[1] that it is worth while paying some attention to this chapter. The people wept when they heard the law, no doubt realizing how greatly they had disobeyed its precepts, and how they deserved the curses that it threatened against the disobedient.

---

[1] For instance, Batten, *Ezra and Nehemiah*, p. 373, "The Law-book of Ezra was not Deuteronomy, but either the priestly law or the whole Pentateuch," and Ed. Meyer, *Papyrusfund von Elephantine*, p. 70. But Torrey says correctly (*Ezra Studies*, p. 262 note) "The laws quoted and accepted in the story [*i.e.* of Ezra] do not belong, as a rule, to the priestly legislation," and van Hoonacker, *Schweich Lectures*, p. 17, "Le Deutéronome, plus que le 'Code sacerdotal,' était la législation en vue à l'époque de Néhémie et d'Ezra."

But Ezra comforted them by telling them that this was a holy day and a day in which they were to rejoice. So they ceased to weep, and began to make merry, and sent portions, as Ezra told them, to the poor. So far there was no mention of the Feast of Booths, nor was it said on what grounds the day was holy; but viii. 13 f. goes on to say that when the Law was read on the second day they heard the directions to dwell in booths in the feast of the seventh month. Straightway the people made themselves booths, and kept the feast seven days. Verse 18 also mentions a solemn assembly on the eighth day.

With the exception of this last verse the whole of the proceedings can be explained as following the legislation of Deuteronomy. The directions for the Feast of Booths are found in Deut. xvi. 13–15 and xxxi. 10–13, both of which passages are regarded by Driver as part of the original Deuteronomic work. No precise date is given for the feast: it was to be held after the harvest. This had been the original practice of JE (Ex. xxiii. 16, xxxiv. 22), when the feast was observed locally, but it would practically have always been in the seventh or the eighth month; and as Deuteronomy insisted on the centralization of the feast the date probably became fixed. I Kings xii. 32, 33, by giving the date of the festival at Bethel as the fifteenth day of the eighth month, and by saying that Jeroboam had devised the month[1] in his own heart, suggests that the festival at Jerusalem was held in the seventh month. This is what we find in

---

[1] The Greek alters "month" into "feast"; but the Hebrew text is supported by the Targum and the Syriac version.

Ezek. xlv. 25 and P (Lev. xxiii. 34, 39, Numb. xxix. 12) where the date is given as the fifteenth day of the seventh month. How can we then account for Ezra having the feast on the second day of the month? Only by supposing that he was following the written Deuteronomic legislation, and did not feel bound by later unwritten tradition. Ezra's story closely follows the Deuteronomic legislation, as is seen by the stress laid upon the rejoicing, the directions to give portions to the poor, and above all to the reading of the Law at this time, and the presence of women and children as well as men. All these are mentioned in Deuteronomy, and there is no mention of any of them in H or P except just a bare reference to rejoicing in Lev. xxiii. 40 (H). Although speaking of the first day of the month as 'holy' Ezra does not use the technical expression "holy convocation" by which P describes it; nor is there any mention of the Feast of Booths as a memorial of the Exodus, which H lays stress on (Lev. xxiii. 43). Moreover, had Ezra been following the legislation of P we should have expected blowing of trumpets on the first day of the month, and a day of fasting, the great Day of Atonement, on the tenth day of the month (Lev. xxiii. 24–32, Numb. xxix. 1–11). With these very serious divergences from the priestly legislation it seems unwise to pre-suppose a dependence on P because of the mention in Neh. viii. 18 of a solemn assembly on the eighth day. This certainly is not mentioned in JE or D, and its mention in H is doubtful[1] (Lev. xxiii. 39), while it is certainly commanded in P (Lev. xxiii. 36, Numb. xxix. 35). It is however possible

[1] Driver and Benzinger think that part of the verse is P.

that the custom had grown up of observing an extra day, and that this custom was followed by Ezra without reference to a law book; but it is much more probable that the Chronicler added the eighth day here to the narrative he found before him, just as he added it in II Chron. vii. 8–10 when copying from I Kings viii. 66. In Kings we are told that Solomon sent the people away on the eighth day; but in II Chron. vii. the eighth day was observed by a solemn assembly. The Chronicler's hand is evident here in Neh. viii. 17 in the statement that there had not been such a celebration of the Feast of Booths since the days of Joshua the son of Nun, which is just parallel with what he said about Josiah's passover in II Chron. xxxv. 18.

Thus there is every reason to believe that the book which Ezra read to the people was none other than the book of Deuteronomy. On the first day he must have read the first fifteen chapters, which contained enough commandments and threats to cause all the weeping of the people. On the second day he began chapter xvi. with its directions for the Feast of Booths, and he encouraged them to hold the feast at once, so as to make them merry and to gain their support in his intended policy of enforcing also the harder injunctions of the law. What has been said does not prove that Ezra *knew* no other law book than the one he read to the people. There is no suggestion in the narrative that he was reading a new book, and it was a matter of the utmost importance, if he was to play any part in developing their legal system, that he should proclaim himself as a champion of the existing law. There was sufficient in Deuteronomy that needed to be enforced before it was necessary to introduce new legislation.

One of the results of the reading of the Law was to emphasize the prohibition against mixed marriages. Nehemiah had previously taken the matter up, and had made offenders swear not to repeat the offence. But if Ezra came to Jerusalem early in the reign of Artaxerxes II it was about thirty years since Nehemiah's attempt to stop the practice, and that allowed plenty of time for a repetition of it. According to Ezr. ix. the matter was brought to Ezra's notice by some of the chiefs. Ezra showed signs of the deepest grief and astonishment when he heard about it, probably having supposed that Nehemiah's action had stamped out the practice once for all. In his prayer which follows he quotes the commandments against mixed marriages as having been given by the prophets (Ezr. ix. 11), referring mainly to the Pentateuch, though perhaps also having Ezekiel in mind. The expression indicates an early date, before the canonization of Torah and Prophets as two separate collections. The direct quotations in verses 11 and 12 come from Deuteronomy, with only slight alterations such as plural for singular—"the land into which ye go to possess it," Deut. vii. 1; "And now give not your daughters to their sons, and take not their daughters for your sons," Deut. vii. 3; "and ye shall not seek their peace and their good for ever," Deut. xxiii. 7 (E.V. 6). But the statement that Palestine "is an unclean land through the uncleanness of the peoples of the lands, through their abominations which have filled it from one end to another with their filthiness" is not a quotation from anywhere in the Pentateuch. The thought appears, it is true, in Lev. xviii. 24–30, but the language is strikingly different, and there can be no question at all here of quotation from that passage. The word used for unclean by Ezra (נִדָּה) is used in Leviticus only in the sense of sexual impurity, and in Numbers only in the sense of the impurity contracted by touching a corpse. The defilement caused by idolatry is described by the term נִדָּה and attributed in Ezek. vii. 19, 20 to the gold of Judah, in Lam. i. 17 to Jerusalem, and in II Chron. xxix. 5 to idolatrous furniture introduced into the temple by Ahaz. It is in such a sense, of defilement caused by idolatry, that Ezr. ix. 11 uses the word, and not in the restricted senses in which it is used in P.

It is to be presumed that Nehemiah, in the action he took against mixed marriages, was also following Deuteronomy. The quotation in Neh. xiii. 1, 2 about the Ammonite and Moabite never entering into the congregation of God is from Deut. xxiii. 4–6 (E.V. 3–5); but that fact does not help us much as the verses are almost certainly from the hand of the Chronicler and not from Nehemiah's Memoirs[1].

As Ezra made his great confession in front of the temple a large congregation of Jews collected (Ezr. x.),

[1] Van Hoonacker, *Schweich Lectures*, p. 16, says "Ce n'est pas le 'Code sacerdotal,' c'est le Deutéronome qui défend les unions avec les femmes étrangères, notamment avec les femmes cananéennes, et c'est aussi au Deutéronome vii. 1—3 qu'on en appelle contre les coupables obstinés Ezra ix. 1—2." König, *Moderne Pentateuch-kritik*, p. 100, says "Die Opposition von Esra und Nehemiah gegen die Mischheiraten (vgl. hauptsächlich die Sätze Esr. ix. 11) stützt sich am direktesten auf Deut. vii. 1, 3, xi. 8, xxiii. 7."

and one of their leaders suggested making a covenant
to divorce all foreign wives and their children. This
proposal was adopted. Nehemiah had only made
offenders promise not to repeat the offence, but Ezra
took the much more drastic step of divorce; and this
supports the theory that Ezra followed Nehemiah.
The Jews collected within three days at Jerusalem in
response to a proclamation, and the shortness of the
period indicates how small the community must have
been at that time. The people agreed to divorce their
foreign wives, but as it was the rainy season it was
decided that a tribunal should be appointed to enquire
into the cases, and that the accused should be sent for
as required and should be accompanied by local repre-
sentatives. The tribunal began its work on the first
day of the tenth month, and finished on the first day
of the first month. Four priests were found guilty, and
undertook to divorce their wives, and paid a fine for
their offence (Ezr. x. 19). Six Levites, four singers
and porters, and nearly a hundred of the people were
also found guilty. I Esdr. ix. 36 says "All these had
taken strange wives, and they put them away with
their children," which is the original conclusion in
place of the unintelligible Hebrew text of Ezr. x. 44.
The list of offenders may seem small, but in a small
community much offence may have been caused by a
few cases, especially if some of them were distinguished
people as is stated in Ezr. ix. 2. A gathering took
place on the twenty-fourth day of the month (Neh. ix.)
when the divorce was formally proclaimed. The greater
part of the chapter consists of a long sermon or address
to God after the style of the book of Judges. The

present text lacks any proper introduction to this
address. Most likely it was attributed to Ezra, though
it is not part of his Memoirs. As it has been suggested
that Neh. ix. and Neh. x. are independent of each other
and have nothing to do with Ezra's covenant, it may
be well to point out that of the ten Levites mentioned
in Neh. ix. 4, 5 seven appear in the list of Levites in
Neh. x. 10–14 (E.V. 9–13); and that of the sixteen
names in this latter list seven also appear in Neh. viii. 7
among the list of those who "caused the people to
understand the law."

Chapter x. starts with a list of people who signed
a covenant, and then gives the terms of the covenant.
Two hands are fairly clearly marked, verses 34, 38–40 a
(E.V. 33, 37–39 a) being additions. The later hand is
undoubtedly the Chronicler. The earlier hand might
quite well be the actual covenant. The terms of the
covenant are given as follows:

(a) Not to intermarry with foreigners, from Deut.
vii. 3.

(b) Not to trade on the sabbath. Work on the
sabbath is prohibited in all the codes. There may be a
reminiscence of Jeremiah or Ezekiel.

(c) To forgo the seventh year, Ex. xxiii. 11 (E),
Deut. xv. 1–11, Lev. xxv. 1–7.

(d) To forgo all debts in the seventh year, Deut. xv. 2.

(e) To pay one-third of a shekel temple tax. This
is found nowhere in the Pentateuch. P orders half a
shekel, Ex. xxx. 13, xxxviii. 26.

(f) To bring in the wood-offering in turn determined by lot. This is also mentioned in Neh. xiii. 31.

As it says that this command was written in the Law we
must suppose that it existed in an earlier edition than
we have. There is no mention of it in our Pentateuch,
though Lev. vi. 5 (E.V. 12) shows that wood was used.

(g) To bring firstfruits:

of ground and fruit of trees, Ex. xxiii. 19 (E),
Deut. xxvi. 2, 10.

of sons and cattle, Ex. xxii. 28, 29 (E.V. 29,
30) (E), xiii. 2 (P), etc.

of herds and flocks, Deut. xii. 6, etc.

(h) Not to forsake the house of God.

After (e) verse 34 (E.V. 33) adds an explanation of
the uses of the temple tax. These are all from P, viz.
shewbread, Lev. xxiv. 5 f.; continual meal offering and
continual burnt offering, Ex. xxix. 38–42; holy things;
and sin offerings, Lev. vii. 37. The other addition
38–40 a (E.V. 37–39 a) betrays itself by starting the
list again after it had been rounded off with the words
"to bring to the house of our God, unto the priests
that minister in the house of our God," and by repeating the firstfruit of the fruit of trees which had already
been mentioned[1]. The coarse meal and heave offerings
which it mentions come from Ezek. xliv. 30 or
Numb. xv. 20 (P). Then it says that tithes are to be
collected in all the cities by the Levites accompanied
by a priest, and one-tenth of the tithes is to be
brought by the Levites to the storehouse in the
temple. This is an interesting provision, and we must
consider the different laws of tithes. Deuteronomy says

[1] Batten suspects v. 34 of being an elaboration by the Chronicler.
Kittel marks vv. 38 b—40 in his *Biblia Hebraica* as an addition.

(1) that the annual tithe (or a money equivalent) was to be brought to the central sanctuary to be eaten there by the whole family and servants and by "the Levite that is within thy gates," Deut. xii. 17–19, xiv. 22–27; and (2) that every third year the whole tithe was to be stored locally as a provision for the local Levites, strangers, fatherless and widows, Deut. xxvi. 12, xiv. 28, 29. The priestly law is different: Lev. xxvii. 30–33 says that all the tithe of every kind is holy unto Yahweh; Numb. xviii. 21–28 says that the whole of the tithe was to be given to the Levites, and they in their turn were to treat this as their income and give a tenth of it as a heave offering "to Aaron the priest," *i.e.* to the priests. It is with the priestly law of tithe that Neh. x. 38–40 is in agreement.

Thus we see that the whole of the original covenant of chapter x., as far as it can be traced, refers to the Deuteronomic law together with E, agreeing with what we have found in the case of the Feast of Booths and the mixed marriages that Ezra was dependent on the earlier legislation, particularly Deuteronomy, and not at all on the priestly code. But the additions to Neh. x. by the Chronicler are almost entirely dependent on P.

Now let us turn back to Nehemiah's action in the matter of tithes. Neh. xiii. 12 does not follow Deuteronomy, for the people neither ate the tithes at the central sanctuary, nor stored them locally for the poor. It is much nearer P, for the people brought the tithes to Jerusalem, there to be distributed by the treasurers to the Levites. There is no mention here however of a tenth of the tithes for the priests, which we do find in

Neh. xii. 47 and xiii. 5 which are not parts of Nehemiah's Memoirs and are probably by the Chronicler. It is therefore probable that in Nehemiah's time the tithes were given straight to the priests at Jerusalem, as is also the arrangement in Ezra's covenant, Neh. x. 37 (E.V. 36)—a distinct development over the earlier Deuteronomic arrangement in which local Levites simply had their share with other poor and landless people—but that at a later time the system was developed, that we find in P and the Chronicler, of giving the whole tithes to the Levites and tithing the Levites for the benefit of the priests.

The system of tithing at the time when the book of Malachi was written was exactly the same as in Nehemiah's time. The people were exhorted to bring the tithe into the storehouse at the house of God (Mal. iii. 10). This change from Deuteronomy is perhaps partly to be explained by supposing that when Deuteronomy was written the Levites lived all over the country (cf. the expression "the Levite that is within thy gates"), but that later, owing to the centralization of the worship, they all came to live in Jerusalem. It was only in the period between Nehemiah's two administrations that the tithes were so neglected that the Levites had to go into the country to earn their living (Neh. xiii. 10). In Malachi, as in Nehemiah's Memoirs, there is no mention of tithing the Levites for the priests. Nor should we expect it, for Malachi draws no distinction between priests and Levites, Mal. ii. 4–8, iii. 3. Ezek. xliv. 10–16 makes it clear that before the Exile the Levites were allowed to exercise priestly functions, but that owing to their apostasy they had been degraded to inferior ministrations, and only the Levites who were the sons of Zadok were to be allowed to perform the priestly function of offering the fat and the blood of the sacrifices. This distinction was adopted later, and is seen repeatedly in P and the Chronicler's writings. P speaks of the valid priests as the sons of Aaron, *e.g.* Lev. xxi. 1. II Chron. xxxv. 10–15 makes the distinction clear: the Levites slew and flayed the animals, and the priests offered the blood. Whether there was any such distinction in the time of Nehemiah and Ezra it is impossible to say, for the Chronicler's revising hand has been busy with little points like that[1]. In P the covenant of an everlasting priesthood was made with Phinehas the son of Aaron (Numb. xxv. 10–13), but in Mal. ii. 5 the covenant was with Levi.

A point of some difficulty in the history of the Law is the composition of altars. JE, which allowed altars anywhere, ordered that they should be made of earth or of unhewn stones. D ordered an altar at the central sanctuary, without specifying its material, *i.e.* presumably continuing the practice of JE. P has two altars of acacia wood, one plated with gold before the Holy of Holies, and one plated with brass, in the court, for burnt offerings. Solomon's altars, according to the book of Kings, were similar. Ezekiel mentions an altar of wood (xli. 22) evidently before the Holy of Holies, and an altar in the court for burnt offerings

---

[1] Wellhausen, *Prolegomena*, p. 142, "Nicht bloss im Deuteronomium, sondern überall im Alten Testament abgesehen von Esdrae Nehemiae und Chronik ist Levit der Ehrentitel des Priesters."

(xliii. 13-17) without specifying the material. Now Ezr. iii. 2, in the account of the erection of the altar in Cyrus' reign, says that they *built* an altar (וַיִּבְנוּ), suggesting an altar of stones, and this is the more striking because the Chronicler, like P, usually speaks of *making* altars (עָשָׂה). It looks very much as if the priestly editor of the Law tried to bring about a change from the old stone altars to a brazen altar, and the change may have been successful for a while, but when we come to Maccabean times we find that they had gone back to the older legislation, for both the desecrated altar which they took down and also the new altar which they set up were made of stones (I Macc. iv. 45-47). One must regard the priestly edition of the Torah as the outcome of a religious movement which attempted to substitute the principles of P for those of the earlier codes. To a considerable extent the movement must have been successful at the time, or these regulations, so often at variance with the existing written law (even if embodying ancient unwritten customs), would never have been admitted into the law book. But they never succeeded in ousting completely the older legislation, with the result that Jews of later generations found themselves in possession of contradictory laws and were free to pick and choose as seemed good in their own eyes.

Papyrus 6, already referred to, gives valuable information about the Feast of the Passover. For it will be remembered that this papyrus does not record the practice of the Jews of Elephantine, but consists of written directions sent to them, apparently from the priests in Jerusalem, in the year 419 B.C. W. R. Arnold, in his important article on this papyrus[1], says "From the limited dimensions of our papyrus, and especially from the distribution of the surviving material, it is quite certain that the papyrus made no reference whatever to the slaying of the passover lamb....In other words, our papyrus related solely to the feast of Unleavened Bread." The probable explanation is that however much the Jerusalem Jews might be willing to shut their eyes to existing practices at Elephantine, they were not likely to authorize a breach of the Deuteronomic law in an official communication. It is true that P (Ex. xii. 7) mitigated the strictness of D (Deut. xvi. 5–7) in allowing the passover to be *eaten* in houses instead of at the central sanctuary, but this did not abrogate the law that the *killing* of the lambs, like all other sacrifices, was to take place at the central sanctuary. When however we come to consider the details that remain on the tattered papyrus we find that, apart from the absence of the sacrifice of lambs, they follow the regulations of P. For the papyrus has first a distinct reference to the fourteenth day, thus אנתם כן מנו ארב... "Count ye thus fou[rteen days]." This is the date on which according to P (Ex. xii. 6) the lambs were slain, and it is not mentioned in JE or D. Then the papyrus mentions the period "from the fifteenth to the twenty-first day of" Nisan. JE and D had mentioned seven days of unleavened bread, but it is only in P that we find specified the actual dates. The fifteenth day fell into the background in

---

[1] "The Passover Papyrus from Elephantine," *Journ. of Bibl. Lit.*, 1912, p. 1. See also Ed. Meyer, *Sitzungsber. d. k. preuss. Akad. d. Wiss.*, 1911, p. 1051 f.

P, the feast of unleavened bread being regarded as part of the passover feast which took place the day before; but the fifteenth day is still mentioned in Numb. xxviii. 17 and Lev. xxiii. 6, though it does not appear in the accounts in Ex. xii. 1–20 and Numb. ix. 2–14, nor in the Chronicler's stories of passovers in II Chron. xxx., xxxv., and Ezr. vi. 19–22. We may then quite rightly follow Prof. Arnold in claiming the "Passover Papyrus" as the first conclusive evidence for the existence as early as 419 B.C. of P or an early section of it—for he attributes Lev. xxiii. 5–8 to H, whereas Driver attributes it to P. We might perhaps go further, and suggest that the promulgation of these regulations marks the beginning of the priestly movement of revising the ancient legislation and bringing it into closer touch with actual practice. It is noteworthy that this movement thus began before the arrival of Ezra, but that would not prevent him from being a leading figure in the movement. The records he has left us certainly give no hint that he was a supporter of the revised legislation. But the time within which the Pentateuch was completed was fairly short, for it must have been complete before the Samaritan schism which took place about 330 B.C. And we have seen enough of Ezra's character to see that he would sympathize with those ritualistic tendencies which mark the priestly code. There is every probability that he played an important part in furthering this work; it may be that he did not do a great deal personally, but that he founded a school of priests who carried the work through.

Jewish tradition connects Ezra with the Great

Synagogue, which was supposed to have filled the
gap between the last of the prophets and Simon the
Just[1]. Whether there ever was such a body as the
Great Synagogue is very doubtful, but it is interesting
to note the three sayings which are attributed to it,
namely, "Be deliberate in judgment, raise up many
disciples, and make a fence round the Law." These
may very well represent the ruling ideas of the religious leaders towards the end of the Persian period.
The second saying suggests the foundation of schools
for priests, and the third one suggests careful devotion
to the study and amplification of the Law. Cowley[2]
draws attention to the passage in Sanhedrin fol. 21 b,
which says, "The Law was originally given to Israel
in Hebrew writing and the holy language. It was
given them again in Ezra's time in Assyrian writing
and the Aramaic language. Israel chose to retain the
Assyrian writing and the holy language, leaving to
the ignorant the Hebrew writing and the Aramaic
language." Cowley thinks that this probably meant
that Ezra transcribed the Law from the cuneiform
character in which it had previously been written into
the square Aramaic character from which the modern
Hebrew character is derived. If that was the case
Ezra's work was very important in popul rizing the
Jewish Law. "Hitherto," writes Cowley, "the Law
had been the peculiar possession of the priestly and
learned class: henceforward it was to be accessible to
everyone who would learn an alphabet."

---

[1] *Pirqe Aboth*, i. 1.

[2] *Journal of Theological Studies*, vol. XI. July 1910, "Ezra's Recension of the Law."

Finally a word must be said about Ezra's existence. Surely no one can read the account of what he did, carrying on a stage further the policy of Nehemiah, without feeling subjectively that it is a story of a real character. But, in truth, the one argument that seemed of any weight against his existence was that he was an invention of the Chronicler, reflecting merely the Chronicler's ideals and opinions. The preceding pages will have dissipated that idea, if they have succeeded in showing that Ezra's recorded actions are based on Deuteronomy whereas the Chronicler is steeped in the ideas of the priestly code.

CHAPTER XI

THE FOURTH CENTURY

FROM Ezra's time in the beginning of the fourth century up to the end of the Persian period there is but scanty information about the history of the Jews. In that century the efforts of the Jews were being devoted to the completion of the Torah, and they had little interest in recording the events of their own days.

A solitary event has been recorded as taking place in the middle of the century. The records of it are scrappy, and commentators have differed widely as to the construction to be placed upon them[1]. Until the discovery of the Aramaic papyri, with their mention of Bagohi as the governor of Judah, this event was frequently confused with Josephus' story of the punishment of the Jews by Bagoses. It was recorded by Eusebius in his Chronicle, which is unfortunately not extant in the original. Two references to it are however known, the one a quotation from the Chronicle by Jerome, and the other the Armenian version of the Chronicle.

Jerome, Olympiad 105. "Ochus apodasmo Judaeorum capta in Hyrcaniam accolas translatos juxta

---

[1] Cheyne, Bampton Lectures, *Origin of the Psalter*, p. 53; also his article "Critical Problems of the second part of Isaiah" in the *Jewish Quarterly Review*, Oct. 1891, p. 108. Judeich, *Kleinasiatische Studien*, pp. 170, 176. Nöldeke, art. "Persia" in *Encycl. Britannica*, 9th edition. Driver, *Introd. to Literature of O.T.*, p. 222.

mare Caspium conlocavit." The statement is dated in different MSS. as the fifth or the sixth year of Ochus, *i.e.* 354–353 B.C. For 'apodasmo' Graetz[1] suggests reading 'Artaxerxes urbe,' thus making the sentence begin "Ochus Artaxerxes, the city of the Jews having been captured,...." It seems however much more likely that Eusebius had written ἀποδασμοῦ, "a portion of the Jews having been captured," which agrees with the Armenian version "partem aliquam."

Armenian Version. "Ochus partem aliquam de Romanis Judaeisque cepit et habitare fecit in Hyrcania juxta mare Cazbium." The statement is dated as the sixth year of Ochus, *i.e.* 353 B.C. For 'Romanis,' which is obviously an error, Graetz proposes to read 'Idumaeis.'

Syncellus gives a longer account. He was probably indebted for his information to Diodorus Siculus whose immediate source was also the Chronicle of Eusebius.

Syncellus (*Dindorf*) i. 486. Ὦχος Ἀρταξέρξου παῖς εἰς Αἴγυπτον στρατεύων μερικὴν αἰχμαλωσίαν εἷλεν Ἰουδαίων, ὧν τοὺς μὲν ἐν Ὑρκανίᾳ κατῴκισε πρὸς τῇ Κασπίᾳ θαλάσσῃ, τοὺς δὲ ἐν Βαβυλῶνι οἳ καὶ μέχρι νῦν εἰσιν αὐτόθι, ὡς πολλοὶ τῶν Ἑλλήνων ἱστοροῦσιν.

The following reference from Solinus may also be intended to refer to the same event.

Solinus xxxv. 4. "Judaeae caput fuit Hierosolyma, sed excisa est. Successit Hiericus, et haec desivit Artaxerxis bello subacta."

The reign of Artaxerxes III, Ochus, was full of wars, in which he tried to hold together the disintegrating

---

[1] "Last Chapter of Zechariah" in the *Jewish Quarterly Review*, Jan. 1891, p. 209.

empire. Egypt, Phoenicia and Cyprus were in revolt. Sidon headed the revolt of Phoenicia, and was supported by 4000 Greek mercenaries from Egypt under Mentor the Rhodian. This was a general revolt of the Syrian satrapies and it is more than likely that Judaea also joined in. Sidon as the leader of the revolt suffered most severely. The town was betrayed through the treachery of its king Tennes and of Mentor, and so desperate was the plight of the inhabitants that, it is said, they burnt their fleet and set fire each man to his own house, 40,000 persons perishing in the fire. Diodorus Siculus xvi. dates the conquest of Phoenicia and Egypt during the years 351 to 348 B.C., but Grote gives reason for thinking that it was not till after 346 B.C.[1] In any case, if Eusebius' date 354 or 353 B.C. for the Jewish captivity is correct, it will be before the fall of Sidon. This is surprising if the captivity was a punishment for participating in the Phoenician revolt, for one would have expected that Ochus would have left the less important countries like Judaea till he had finished with Sidon. But it is possible that it took some time to prepare. the great army with which he advanced against Tennes king of Sidon and his ally Mentor, and that during this interval one of his generals, who was operating against Egypt, subdued Judaea on his way. One of the noted Persian generals at that time was Orophernes, and it has been conjectured that it was he who commanded the section of the army which attacked Judaea, and that dim memories of the occasion gave rise to the story of Holofernes in the book of Judith.

[1] *History of Greece*, XI. p. 609.

It will be seen that the evidence we have is sufficient to make it very probable that Judaea suffered at
this time at the hands of Ochus or one of his generals.
There is however no evidence that the suffering of
Jerusalem was anything so great that it could be
described as a national disaster, "the third of Israel's
great captivities" as Cheyne called it. There is no
other evidence to support Solinus' statement about
the destruction of Jerusalem and Jericho.

Josephus[1] relates a series of incidents as happening
at the time of Alexander the Great. Sanballat, a
Cuthean, of the same stock as the Samaritans, was
sent by Darius III to Samaria, and gave his daughter
Nicaso in marriage to Manasseh, brother of Jaddua
the high-priest of Jerusalem. The Jewish elders were
incensed at this union, and ordered Manasseh either
to divorce Nicaso or not to approach the altar.
Manasseh thereupon offered to divorce his wife, but
Sanballat said he would build a temple on Mt Gerizim
and make Manasseh high-priest there, besides giving
him authority over all places under his rule. This
arrangement suited Manasseh well, and other priests
and Levites from Jerusalem went and joined him, and
were given land in Samaria. Alexander defeated
Darius at Issus and marched against Tyre. When he
arrived outside Tyre he sent to the Jewish high-priest
for auxiliaries and supplies, which Jaddua refused on
the grounds of his oath of allegiance to Darius. Sanballat, seeing his opportunity, came to Tyre with
eight thousand Samaritans whose services he offered
to Alexander. Alexander received him and granted

[1] *Ant.* XI. vii. 2–viii. 7, and XIII. ix. 1.

him his request to build a temple on Mt Gerizim. After the capture of Tyre and Gaza Sanballat died. Alexander advanced against Jerusalem. Jaddua, following the instructions he had received in a dream, went out in procession with the priests and citizens of Jerusalem to meet Alexander. The great conqueror was so much impressed by the scene, remembering a dream he had had while yet in Macedonia, that he adored the name of God which was engraved on the high-priest's breast-plate and saluted the high-priest. He entered Jerusalem, and offered sacrifice in the temple according to the high-priest's directions, and granted the Jews to live under their own laws, and remitted from them all tribute on the seventh year. The Samaritans then asked Alexander to grant them also remittance of tribute on the seventh year, but he refused to grant it till he had made further enquiries. He then sent the troops which Sanballat had given him to Upper Egypt to garrison the country of the Thebaid.

Now it is recorded in Neh. xiii. 28 that Sanballat, the governor of Samaria in Nehemiah's time, gave his daughter in marriage to one of the sons of Joiada the son of Eliashib the high-priest. It is most unlikely that in two different periods there were governors of Samaria named Sanballat who gave their daughters in marriage to members of the high-priestly family at Jerusalem, and there can be little doubt that Josephus borrowed this incident from Neh. xiii. 28, only mistakenly connected it with the events of Alexander's time. This does not necessarily invalidate the rest of his narrative; and it is quite likely that the latter part of the narrative is based upon facts. We may take it as probable, until further evidence for or against appears, that Alexander did not attack Jerusalem but treated the Jews leniently and permitted them to live under their own laws, and that he permitted the Samaritans to build a temple on Mt Gerizim. It is quite likely that the first high-priest of this temple was named Manasseh, for this is probably the force of the Massoretic tradition which substituted 'Manasseh' for 'Moses' as the ancestor of the line of priests at Dan in Judg. xviii. 30. A possible reference to the fact that Alexander stayed his hand and did not attack Jerusalem may be seen in Zech. ix. 8, "And I will encamp over against my house, an outpost, that none may pass to or fro." The preceding verses are a poetical prophecy announcing the imminent fall of Phoenicia and the Philistine towns before Alexander. This verse is in prose, and seems to be an addition by a later hand to make the prophecy tally more fully with the fulfilment.

If we follow Josephus provisionally in dating the Samaritan schism in the time of Alexander, this will also give us a provisional date for the completion of the Pentateuch. It is not very likely that after the schism they would have accepted a totally new book, but they might have accepted a revision of the Pentateuch if they had the book already. Montgomery says[1], "From all we know of Samaritanism there can be no doubt that it remained under the steady influence of Judaism, and that this spiritual patronage was so strong and so necessary that even after the

[1] *Samaritans*, pp. 72, 73.

complete excommunication of the schismatics in the third and fourth Christian centuries Rabbinism still infiltrated into Samaria."..."In any case we know too little of the relations between the Jews and the Samaritans for at least 200 years to say that the Pentateuch could not have been further revised after the schism, on the ground that the Samaritan copy would give a much older and different text. It is possible that further revisions at Jerusalem, as in the case of Ex. xxxv.–xl., were readily accepted by the spiritually dependent community at Shechem. But with the Jewish promulgation of the Second Canon, that of the Prophets, about 200, a definite break must have separated the two sects on the question as to the extent of Scripture. The northern community could not accept the Second Canon with its pronounced proclivities for Juda, David, and Jerusalem."

CHAPTER XII

TENDENCIES AND CONTROVERSIES

IT is not intended in this last chapter to deal with every phase of thought which found prominent expression during our period. Some of them are more fitly dealt with in connexion with other periods. For instance, a writer on apocalyptic Judaism would not ignore the beginnings of apocalyptic thought that are to be found in Zechariah, but it is in the light of the great apocalyptic writers of later periods that the full significance is seen of the germs sown by Zechariah. Likewise with the Messianic idea. It is not convenient to treat separately that section of it which falls between the years 538 and 333 B.C. It was a process of thought commencing probably as early as Isaiah if not earlier, and continuing up to its culmination in the coming of Christ, and even after His advent filling an important place in Jewish and Samaritan thought, as well as becoming retrospectively a significant element of Christian theology. To attempt to deal separately with the portion of Messianic thought that falls in the Persian period would be rather like trying to deal with the structure and functions of a tree trunk without at the same time dealing with the root and leaves. It is otherwise with the two tendencies, commonly described by the names Legalism and Particularism, which, though germinating earlier, reached a stage within our period sufficiently developed to bear fruit in the immediately succeeding generations.

An ideal of world-wide universalism was set, as we have seen, by Deutero-Isaiah in the task that he laid before Israel of becoming the missionary of Yahweh among the nations. The author of Is. lxvi., possibly the same man as Deutero-Isaiah, set an ideal of freedom from ritual, saying that God needed neither a house nor a sacrificial cultus, but looked at the hearts of men. The leaders of Jewish thought whose work we have already considered seem to have gone directly counter to both these ideals. Instead of welcoming the nations into the religion of Yahweh, they first rejected the Samaritans who requested to be allowed to share in it, and then they developed that national particularism which manifested itself in the prohibition of intermarriage with foreigners. The limit is reached in P's account of the slaughter of the Midianites in Numb. xxxi. The men were all slain in battle, and when the rest were brought in as captives Moses commanded that all the male children and married women were to be slain in cold blood. H. P. Smith[1] says, "There seems to be no historic basis for the story; it only embodies the author's idea of the way in which the Israel of the future will deal with the heathen." In the manner of their worship the leaders of Jewish thought preferred to follow Ezekiel rather than Isaiah and Deutero-Isaiah. First they built a temple at Jerusalem to be His exclusive dwelling, and then they developed and enforced the ritual side of religion till it culminated towards the end of our

[1] *Religion of Israel*, p. 235.

period in the completion of the Pentateuch with the ritualistic bias of the priestly code.

Though this was the dominating character of the religion of the period we must not suppose that the opposing aspects of religion were altogether dead. Indeed several records remain of a type of religion more in accordance with the teaching of Deutero-Isaiah.

The most remarkable of these records, the book of Jonah, is a satire on the official attitude of the Jews towards the Gentiles. Jonah, typical of the Jews of the time, received a direct message from God to go and preach repentance to the Gentile city of Nineveh. He refused to do so, just as the Jewish nation was refusing the call of Deutero-Isaiah to the missionary task. His refusal was based upon a fear that the people of Nineveh would repent and be saved from the wrath of God. With his own mouth he confessed (Jonah i. 9) that Yahweh, the God whom he served, was the creator of sea and land, and yet he felt it intolerable that the people of Nineveh should be allowed the opportunity of repentance and be accepted with favour by God. God taught him the truth by the parable of the gourd. Jonah was angry at the destruction of the gourd, although he had done nothing for it. Should not Yahweh, who had created and cared for the people of Nineveh, have pity on that great city of 120,000 souls and deliver them from their ignorance? (iv. 10, 11). The writer leaves the question unanswered for the inconsistency of the Jewish attitude to be seen and felt. The Jews asserted the sovereignty of Yahweh over the whole universe,

14—2

but refused to draw the conclusion that rightly and logically followed.

Another author who tried to follow some of the teaching of Deutero-Isaiah has left us a short prophecy in Zech. ix. 1–10. Mitchell dates this passage soon after the battle of Issus (333 B.C.) in face of the imminent fall of Sidon, and of Tyre which had withstood previous conquerors, and of the cities of Philistia. The prophet declares, not only that all these cities will be destroyed, but that they will become part of Yahweh's land. Verse 1 probably read originally "The oracle of the word of Yahweh: it shall fall in the land of Hadrak; and Damascus shall be its resting place. For the cities of Aram belong to Yahweh, and Hamath also which bordereth thereon, and Sidon though she is very wise[1]." Then after describing in verse 5 the destruction of Ashkelon, Gaza, and Ekron, the writer comes in verse 6 to Ashdod, and says, "And bastards shall dwell in Ashdod. And I will cut off the pride of the Philistines. And I will take away their blood out of their mouths and their abominations from between their teeth. And they shall become a remnant for our God; and they shall be as a clan in Judah, even Ekron like the Jebusites." In the above translation 'bastards' is a singular used collectively, and similarly the suffixes 'their blood,' 'their mouth,' etc. are singular suffixes used collectively. The word מַמְזֵר 'bastard' only occurs once elsewhere in the Old Testament, Deut. xxiii. 3 (E.V. 2), where such a person may not enter the congregation of Yahweh to the tenth gene-

---

[1] See Mitchell *ad loc.*

ration, and the same is said in the following verse of
Ammonites and Moabites. It seems therefore likely
that the term was used, not of an illegitimate child,
but of the half-castes from mixed Jewish and non-
Jewish marriages. This is supported by the fact that
the word is used in the Mishna in connexion with
Cutheans and Nethinim (Kethuboth iii. 1), and in
connexion with Nethinim alone (Makkoth iii. 1,
Yebamoth ii. 4). By Cutheans the Talmud means
Samaritans. There were probably no Nethinim in
Talmudic times, and the authors had in mind their
foreign origin. Compare also Masseketh Kuthim 27
in which Samaritan bastards are spoken of[1]. Van
Hoonacker thinks that the word מַמְזֵר was added in

Deut. xxiii. 3 in the time of Nehemiah with special
reference to Samaritans[2]. It should not however be
restricted to the Samaritans, but must include all
those of partly Jewish and partly Gentile descent.
The writer of Zech. ix. 6 then holds out a hope of
salvation for such as these, a hope which had been
denied them by Nehemiah and Ezra. They are to be
exiled to Philistia, and there to be cleansed from the
heathenish practices into which they have fallen,
eating flesh with the blood and sacrificing "abominations," i.e. unclean animals. Thus purified they are
to be admitted as a clan of Judah, as the Jebusites,
according to the more probable narrative, had been
(cf. Josh. xv. 63, Judg. i. 21).

[1] Quoted by Montgomery, *Samaritans*, p. 203.
[2] *Schweich Lectures*, p. 17, and *Les Douze Petits Prophètes*, Zech.
ix. 6.

Zech. ix. 9, 10 is a Messianic passage, combining the well-known description of the Messiah as a victorious king with one of the features—the lowliness—of the Servant of Yahweh of Deutero-Isaiah. This Messianic king will "speak peace to the nations," but coming in a Messianic passage this is not really so significant of the feeling of the writer towards other nations as is his more matter-of-fact statement in verses 6 and 7.

Yet another writer holds out a hope of non-Israelites entering the commonwealth of Israel in Is. lvi. 1–8. He seems to be referring to Gentiles who as eunuchs or in any other capacity had attached themselves to Jewish families in Babylonia and wished to return with their patrons to Judaea, but feared that in the narrow exclusiveness of Jerusalem no place would be found for them. Or he may mean to distinguish two different classes, Jewish eunuchs who might fear exclusion from the sanctuary, and Gentile proselytes. The writer encourages such people, by telling them that they will by no means be separated from the people of Yahweh. The only condition is that they must observe the law of Yahweh. One of the most marked outward observances, which had distinguished Jews in exile from the other nations amongst whom they dwelt, was the abstinence from work on the sabbath day. This therefore was made the chief condition of acceptance. It is perhaps surprising to find this emphasis on an external observance side by side with the protest against particularism, but the two tendencies do not necessarily go together. Similar stress on the sabbath is found in Is. lviii. 13, 14, and also in the priestly code in Ex. xxxi. 13, 14 and Numb. xv. 32–36. In the last named passage the offence of breaking the sabbath is regarded as so serious that death is put forward as the proper penalty—not that it is likely that such a penalty was ever exacted. The writer of Is. lvi. 1–8 goes on to say that these eunuchs and strangers are to be accepted within the house of God. Their sacrifices will be accepted; and the house of God will be called "A house of prayer for all peoples." The passage is very important, because the writer is not theorizing, but dealing with an actual case that has arisen, and dealing with it in the true spirit of Deutero-Isaiah. He welcomes these strangers, not as a compromise in a difficult situation, but as the firstfruits of the nations who have a right, when they choose to claim it, in the temple of Jerusalem. Verse 8 is an interpretation, and doubtless the correct one, of what Deutero-Isaiah meant by saying that Israel the Servant of Yahweh was tô restore Israel: the Israel at present gathered was only part of the true Israel, "An oracle of the Lord Yahweh, who gathereth the outcasts of Israel: Yet will I gather (others) unto him in addition to those of his that are gathered."

To the same school of thought belonged the author of Ruth. Even standing by itself it is a story of peculiar charm; but the historical setting of the period of Nehemiah and Ezra invests the author with an heroic daring. He has chosen for his principal character Ruth a Moabitess, of that tribe with which according to Deut. xxiii. 4–6 (E.V. 3–5) no Israelite might marry "till the tenth generation," or according

to the narrower school of the Chronicler "for ever"
(Neh. xiii. 1). Ruth is represented as showing the
utmost piety towards her mother-in-law, and returning
with her to Judah with the words "thy people shall be
my people, and thy God my God" (Ruth i. 16). She
became the wife of Boaz, by whom she was the ances-
tress of David. The people of Bethlehem blessed her
with the words, "The Lord make this woman that is
come into thy house like Rachel and like Leah, which
two did build the house of Israel" (Ruth iv. 11)—a
gentle reminder that even Jacob's wives were foreigners, Aramaeans. There can be little doubt that
Ruth was written with the avowed object of resisting
the narrow nationalist policy of Nehemiah and Ezra.

It is exceptionally difficult to assign definite dates to
the Psalms. They were composed either for personal
or congregational use, and reflect more often personal
religious experiences than the historical events of
the time. Historical references, if they existed, may
have been pruned away or altered to make the hymns
suitable for other occasions. It will be well however,
in spite of this uncertainty, to look at the psalms
which are probably to be placed within the Persian
period, because they reflect the feelings of ordinary
folk rather than of the religious officials. It is noteworthy that these psalms do not lay the stress on the
sacrificial cultus that is seen in Ezra and the priestly
code. Some even dare to echo the words of earlier
prophets who said that Yahweh did not really care
about sacrifices. The writer of Ps. xl. 7–9 (E.V. 6–8),
after saying that Yahweh has not asked for sacrifices,
expresses his readiness to perform the revealed will

of God. Ps. l. is an attack on those who thought they were obeying the commandment of God by offering sacrifices, though all the while they went on in wicked ways. This error arose through an imperfect conception of God, "Thou thoughtest that I was like thee" (v. 21). Ps. li. 18–21 (E.V. 16–19) asserts that Yahweh will only be pleased with sacrifices for sin when they are offered in the true spirit of contrition.

Of greater importance for our purpose are those psalms which show a more generous feeling towards other nations than was officially adopted in post-exilic Judah. Mention has already been made[1] of the Asaph Psalms and their interest in the Northern tribes, and it was suggested that Ps. lxxx. actually had its origin amongst the Samaritans. Cheyne characterized Pss. lxxvii., lxxviii., lxxx. and lxxxi. as "a fine monument of the Pan-Israelitish sentiment of the Persian period[2]." Ps. lxxxi. 4–6 (E.V. 3–5) mentions the feasts of the new moon and the full moon, and specially says that they were ordained for Joseph—the northern tribes. Ps. xxii. is written very largely in the spirit of Deutero-Isaiah, and probably is dependent on his writings. The speaker in the psalm is the Suffering Servant of Yahweh, though the term 'Servant' is not actually employed. As a result of deliverance from all his troubles the sufferer will declare the name of God among his brethren. Jacob and Israel will praise him. All nations shall come and worship Yahweh, to whose dominion all the kingdoms of the world rightly belong. Other, more incidental, references to the conversion of the Gentiles are found

[1] P. 105 ff.   [2] Bampton Lectures, p. 148.

in Ps. lxv. 3 (E.V. 2) "unto thee shall all flesh come,"
lxviii. 32 (E.V. 31) "Princes shall come out of Egypt;
Ethiopia shall haste to stretch out her hands unto
God," lxxxvi. 9 "All nations whom thou hast made
shall come and worship before thee, O Lord; and they
shall glorify thy name," but it is not certain that all
these were written before the end of the Persian
period. The following references show an interest in
other nations, and a hope of including them within
the dominion of Yahweh, but the note is rather that
of extending Yahweh's glory than of bringing good
news of salvation to the Gentiles:—Ps. xcvi. 3 "Declare His glory among the nations, His marvellous
works among all the peoples," xcix. 1–3 "The Lord
reigneth; let the peoples tremble. He sitteth upon
the cherubim; let the earth be moved. Yahweh is
great in Zion and high above all the peoples," and xlvii.
9, 10 (E.V. 8, 9) "God reigneth over the nations. God
sitteth upon His holy throne. The princes of the
people assemble with[1] the people of the God of
Abraham. For the shields of the earth belong unto
God. Greatly exalted is He."

Bertholet's book *Die Stellung der Israeliten und der
Juden zu den Fremden* gives an exceptionally good
account of the history of the attitude of Israelites
towards foreigners. He quotes a number of passages
from JE to show that from the earliest times there
was a distinct aversion on natural grounds to foreign
alliances. He says, "Abraham made Eliezer swear

---

[1] The Hebrew text has עַם 'people'; the Greek has עִם 'with.'
Read עִם עַם ' with the people.'

not to take a Canaanite wife for his son (Gen. xxiv. 3, 37). Aaron and Miriam were obliged to call Moses to account for having taken an Ethiopian wife (Numb. xii. 1). When Samson wanted to marry a daughter of the Philistines his parents protested against it in word and deed, for according to the original narrative they did not even go with him to the marriage (Judg. xiv. 1 ff.). Finally, when the Israelites committed whoredom in Shittim with the daughters of Moab it entangled them in rank idolatry, and resulted in bringing on them the wrath of Yahweh (Numb. xxv. 1–5)[1]." From the time of the prophets and Deuteronomy a new idea appears: "In Deuteronomy Israel receives its constitution, and by that constitution is henceforth separated essentially from other peoples[2]." The opposition to foreigners which had originally been purely national now appears as a religious matter. It is for fear of contamination with heathen religion that the Jews must keep clear of the heathen, and it is with this spirit that the writer of Lam. i. 10 says "The heathen have entered into her sanctuary, concerning whom thou didst command that they should not enter into thy congregation." This tendency became still stronger during the exile; but at the same time a new condition arose when certain 'gerim,' or Gentiles sojourning amongst the Israelites, went into captivity with them, and were bound to them closer by their common experience. "Jeremiah expected in the future the accession of foreigners beyond the bounds of nation and country to the religion of Yahweh....He also created the

[1] Bertholet, *op. cit., p.* 81.   [2] P. 87.

possibility of realizing this ideal by his discovery of the individual as the subject of religion. But we must add that he never supposed that proselytes would be made in the present time. It seemed to him unnatural that a people should give up its God (ii. 11)[1]." With Deutero-Isaiah this possibility became a direct call from God: "Deutero-Isaiah is not satisfied with leaving Israel a passive spectator while its God carries out the work of conversion; rather He allots Israel a positive vocation in the work....With unmistakable clearness it is here declared that Israel has to fulfil a missionary task. It is not to separate itself from the world, not to set its light under the bushel but on the candle-stick[2]." And again further on he says, "We can frame this problem in these words: If the Jews have once become conscious of the world-embracing meaning of their religion, what are the hindrances to prevent them from making it the common property of the whole world, *i.e.* from opening the doors to every man who wished, that he might enter their religious community?[3]"

These quotations from Bertholet show well the condition of thought at the commencement of our period, and the summary of Deutero-Isaiah's message agrees closely with what has been said in Chapter I about Israel's missionary vocation. We have seen that that idea was not dead during the period, being witnessed to by Jonah, Ruth, Zech. ix., Is. lvi., and certain passages from the Psalter; but that the official attitude was altogether opposed to it.

Attempts have been made to justify the official

[1] P. 116.   [2] P. 119.   [3] P. 122.

failure to carry out the ideals of Deutero-Isaiah. Hamilton, after referring to earlier prophets like Amos and Jeremiah, says, "The reason why they were not universalists is not far to seek. There was a certain logical coherence and consistency about their mono-Yahwism which the adoption of a universalist conception such as this would have thrown into utter confusion. It is not too much to say that if they had ceased to believe in the exclusive privileges of Israel, they would soon have ceased to be monotheists[1]." This is hard to understand. One would have thought that to believe in a universal God who only had interest in one particular race showed logical inconsistency; and it can safely be asserted that the monotheism of Deutero-Isaiah and his followers suffered in no whit from their attitude towards the Gentiles.

Montefiore says[2], "Nor must we forget that it was far easier for Deutero-Isaiah and his disciples to contemplate in Babylonia a mission to the gentiles and a close alliance with converted heathens, than for anything of the sort to be enacted upon Judaean soil. The advocates of separatism and exclusiveness had many arguments upon their side." There is undoubtedly some truth in this, but it must be remembered that the disciples of Deutero-Isaiah whom we have quoted were Judaeans and not Babylonians.

Similar arguments may be applied to the question whether the Jews of the post-exilic period were justified in binding their religion, which Deuteronomy had declared to be a religion of the heart, within

[1] H. F. Hamilton, *The People of God*, vol. I., p. 70.
[2] Hibbert Lectures, p. 292.

ritual barriers. And it is only fair to quote in support
of their attitude a justification of a similar process
in another religion. J. H. Moulton, in his *Early
Zoroastrianism*[1], says, "My main contention is that
the *ritual* of the Vendidad was alien to Zarathushtra,
who, as I understand him, had nothing of the ritual or
the sacerdotal in his system. But I have no doubt
that without their adaptation Zarathushtra's thought
would have failed to survive." Similarly H. P. Smith
says of Judaism[2], "The imageless worship of Yahweh
was more elevated than the idolatry to which the
whole Gentile world was addicted. Humanly speaking,
it could not have been preserved pure unless it had
been guarded by ritual barriers."

But Deutero-Isaiah was not "humanly speaking"
when he announced Israel's divine vocation. Nor can
we discuss religious problems "humanly speaking."
Conversion, by which we mean not merely a change
of belief but a change of life and purpose, and similar
religious experiences, are humanly impossible, and
divinely possible, as anyone of pastoral experience
knows. It is a canon of Old Testament criticism that
prophets spoke to their own contemporaries. Deutero-
Isaiah was speaking, not of what was possible in the
far-off days of the Messiah, but of what was possible in his own days. And if any prophet spoke
by inspiration of the Holy Spirit of God he did. And
moreover, the fact that his views still found eloquent
expression in the succeeding centuries, under the conditions of life in Palestine, shows that they were not
outrageously impossible. It can only be a matter for

[1] P. 301, note.   [2] *Religion of Israel*, p. 211.

the profoundest regret that those disciples of his should have been in the minority and unable to shape the policy of nascent Judaism. It is difficult to say how different the history of Christianity might have been if Christ had found the nation, which was to form His cradle, already devoted to the evangelization of the world.

Montefiore says[1], "While on the one hand it was an ethical and spiritual loss that the doctrine of conscious self-sacrifice taught in Is. liii. was not more widely developed and inculcated by the synagogue, the loss was to some extent obliterated by a compensatory gain. For Judaism avoided all those ethical troubles and difficulties involved in theories of vicarious atonement and imputed righteousness which have so largely followed from the teaching of Paul and of the Epistle to the Hebrews." Was it so? Was it really an advantage even to Judaism to burke the difficulty, and to fail to ask by what means sins are forgiven on the Day of Atonement which repentance on any other day of the year is insufficient to cover?[2] And is it not true that the difficulties into which some Christian writers have fallen in attempting to explain the efficacy of the self-sacrifice of Christ have largely been caused by trying to explain that death in terms of the system of ritual sacrifices?

It is noteworthy that Christ goes back in His

[1] Hibbert Lectures, p. 523 f.
[2] See Oesterley and Box, *Religion of the Synagogue*, p. 420. ff. *Yoma* VIII. 8 says "Repentance atones for light offences, both commands and prohibitions, but with regard to heavy offences it leaves them hanging in the balance until the Day of Atonement comes and atones for them."

teaching behind the enactments of the Law to the prophetic teaching. When He said "It was said by them of old time...but I say unto you..." He was claiming the right of prophetic utterance to outweigh the written words of the Law. It was a loss which cannot be overestimated that prophecy ceased in Israel for three centuries. The loss was even felt by Joel (ii. 28, 29) who looked forward to a time when prophecy should be general; but by the time of the Maccabees prophecy had long ceased, and people only looked forward in a vague way to the restoration of the prophetic gift, I Macc. ix. 27, iv. 46, xiv. 41. The advent of Christ restored prophecy. People at once recognized the fact, and hailed John the Baptist as the long foreseen prophet Elijah. Jesus Himself was commonly believed to be a prophet until it was known that He was the Messiah. St Peter, on the birthday of the Church, declared that Joel's words of the outpouring of the gift of prophecy were fulfilled (Acts ii. 14–21).

It is interesting to note a tendency in modern Judaism also to go behind the Law to the prophetic attitude. Montefiore quite recently has said[1], "Modern English Judaism, while not abandoning the Law, is yet, especially in its Reform and Liberal phases, becoming less legal and more prophetic. It is doing this in its own way, and on its own lines....Perhaps the change is partly unconscious. But it is nevertheless going on."

Christ quoted the universalistic hopes of Deutero-Isaiah when He preached in the synagogue at Naz-

---

[1] C. G. Montefiore, "Modern Judaism," *Hibbert Journal*, July 1919.

areth, and declared that they were now fulfilled
(Lk. iv. 17–21). He quoted with approval the universalistic statement that the temple should be called a
house of prayer for all the nations (Mk. xi. 17). He
dealt kindly with the Samaritans, even making a
Samaritan the hero of one of His parables, and in
speaking to a Samaritan woman He said, just in the
spirit of Is. lxvi., "The hour cometh when neither in
this mountain, nor in Jerusalem, shall ye worship the
Father...the hour cometh and now is, when the true
worshippers shall worship the Father in spirit and
truth: for such doth the Father seek to be His worshippers" (John iv. 21–23). When asked for a sign
He reminded them of Jonah (Mt. xvi. 4), but even
the disciples did not understand the reference, for they
had forgotten what the book of Jonah stood for.
St Stephen quoted Is. lxvi. 1 as showing that God
did not need a man-built house to dwell in (Acts vii.
48–50). St Paul's teaching about the law was remarkable, for he realized that the promises of God came
first and the law afterwards. He tried to believe that
the law was a $\pi\alpha\iota\delta\alpha\gamma\omega\gamma\delta\varsigma$ leading to Christ (Gal. iii.
24). He found it difficult to place the law in any
ordered scheme of development, and spoke of it as
having come in adventitiously, $\pi\alpha\rho\epsilon\iota\sigma\tilde{\eta}\lambda\theta\epsilon\nu$, Rom. v.
20. The writer of the Epistle to the Hebrews, who
had more interest in the sacrificial cultus than any
other Christian writer, proclaims that the sacrifices
and offerings were taken away that the will of God
might be done, "He taketh away the first that he may
establish the second," Heb. x. 5–9.

Thus we see that Christianity took those elements

which in early Judaism were had in dishonour, and built them into the framework of a universal religion of the one Father to be worshipped everywhere in spirit and in truth; while those other elements which had the ascendancy in nascent Judaism could not be assimilated into a world-wide religion, and remain in post-Christian Judaism as a memorial and a proof of the rejection by the Jews of their missionary vocation. Let us cast our eyes abroad, and see how large a part of humanity has not yet heard the gospel of Christ, and beware lest we also fall into the same condemnation.

INDEX OF SCRIPTURE AND OTHER
PASSAGES

The references are to the chapter and verse of the Hebrew text.

INDEX

For EU product safety concerns, contact us at Calle de José Abascal, 56–1°,
28003 Madrid, Spain or eugpsr@cambridge.org.

www.ingramcontent.com/pod-product-compliance
Ingram Content Group UK Ltd.
Pitfield, Milton Keynes, MK11 3LW, UK
UKHW020318140625
459647UK00018B/1928